AMERICAN SPIRIT

LAWRENCE M. MILLER

Behavior Management:
The New Science of Managing People at Work

AMERICAN SPIRIT

VISIONS OF A NEW CORPORATE CULTURE

LAWRENCE M. MILLER

William Morrow and Company, Inc.
New York / 1984

Library of Congress Catalog Card Number: 84-60205

ISBN: 0-688-03789-5

Printed in the United States of America

First Edition

1 2 3 4 5 6 7 8 9 10

BOOK DESIGN BY RICHARD ORIOLIO

ACKNOWLEDGMENTS

This book is the product of the past fourteen years of fully enjoyed workaholism, travel, and periodic obsessive behavior. It is primarily the result of my opportunity to observe hundreds of managers at their places of work, an opportunity that would have been impossible if it was not for the heroic tolerance of my wife, Carole, and my children, Lang, Natasha, and Layli.

The writing of a book such as this is a mere data dump. The more difficult task is the data aquisition. The ideas expressed in this book have many origins and many individuals have contributed their thoughts, feedback, and examples.

The origin of this work is personal, not professional or scientific. Over the past number of years I have struggled to integrate my understanding of the transformations taking place in American management and my beliefs about the nature of man and the larger flow of human history. The writings of the Baha'i Faith served as a major source of inspiration, providing a model of an alternative relationship between man, institutions, and society.

My colleagues have suffered through dozens of what must have been unbearable dissertations on conceptual models, most of which were tossed overboard. Tom Werner served as a particularly good ear. Jennifer Howard was always the most practical-minded and helped me keep at least one foot on terra firma. Randa Wilbur and Jane Porter were most helpful in their feedback and reinforcement. Bob Lorber has served as a constant source of moral support and encouragement. It is unlikely that I would have begun the long journey that has led to this book were it not for the very early help of Ralph E. James, Jr., and Ed and Marti Itkin.

Bonnie Barnes, on her summer internship from the Wharton Business School, provided the most detailed and helpfully critical feedback on the manuscript. Dr. Tom Brown at Honeywell, Inc., was also extremely helpful and encouraging in his editorial feedback. Steve Rexford contributed in a similar fashion.

Perhaps the most credit is due to those managers who have had the courage and foresight to initiate and manage effectively a culture change process within their firms. They have taken into full account the values and spirit they wish to instill within their organizations. Perhaps the most impressive change I was associated with has been that at the Continental Can Company. Steve Rexford, Armand Zazueta, and Greg Horrigan deserve full credit for planning and sweating through a change in values, behavior and culture so thorough as to convince the most skeptical. Nevius Curtis, CEO of Delmarva Power, helped me believe that some top managers are genuinely pursuing the integration of their most lofty values with the effective management of their businesses. Warde Wheaton and other executives at Honeywell also served as excellent models.

I owe Spencer Johnson and Ken Blanchard a special thanks for convincing me that writing (and reading) may be useful and influential without being tedious.

CONTENTS

INTRODUCTION

What is lacking in the frenzy to find new management practices
is an examination of the soul and spirit of management, the
foundation upon which management's right to manage rests.

As I left the Exxon Building, I felt the blanket of Houston's August
heat and humidity surrounding me with awesome force. It merely
intensified my dissatisfaction. There was something unfair and un-
controllable at work. I had spent the day with one of Exxon's vice-
presidents, a young and extremely dedicated executive whom I
admired. Despite his twelve-hour days, his intelligence and energy,
he was suffering punishment from above and below. It was the time
of gas lines, oil shortages, and accusations of deficiencies of character
directed at the senior executives of the most visible oil firms.

My firm had been employed to assist in an effort to improve the
productivity and job satisfaction of the headquarters staff. As was
our pattern, I was helping the executives evaluate and change their
own management style while also assisting in the training in and the
implementation of new practices in lower echelons.

The vice-president was caught in a vise similar to that of many
other executives. He read widely and had accepted the challenge to
change the culture of his organization. He understood the necessity
of developing a culture that would result in more involvement and
recognition for subordinates. Yet, if he pursued this change in his
own behavior, he would contradict the accepted style of his successful superiors. He was being pressured to change by his subordinates, his own beliefs, and his strategic understanding of corporate
productivity. However, he was confronted daily with the contradictions of style on the part of his superiors, contradictions that made
everyone question whether or not his efforts had any hope of lasting
beyond his predicted temporary tour of duty. Worse yet, those who
were contradicting his style were in a position to judge his future.

The differences in beliefs between this young executive and his superiors was the gap between generations: They acted on different values, different assumptions about the roles of managers and subordinates.

The cab drivers of Houston provide their own variety of Old West entertainment between the center of the city and the airport. The thrill was sufficient to help me forget that I had left my client in a state of conflict no less severe than when I arrived. Once in the comfort of the plane, I attempted to ignore my own dissatisfaction by retreating to the pages of one of the then-popular books on Japanese management. My dissatisfaction increased. Japan, Japan, Japan! If I read one more word about Japanese management, I would scream. Neither the executives of Exxon, nor those of any other of our clients would adopt the mold of the Japanese.

After fourteen years of assisting America's best corporations in their efforts to improve productivity, I had full confidence in our management techniques but decreasing confidence that any management technique alone was sufficient to the task. My colleagues and I had implemented performance improvement efforts in manufacturing and sales organizations of 3M, American Express, Ford Motor Company, and about a hundred other firms. We knew that by increasing involvement, positive reinforcement, and feedback we could better productivity in most organizations. However, those techniques, as much as they improved performance in the operations, were not adequate to address the more fundamental questions facing American management. Managers were facing a crisis of self-confidence, a questioning of the basic beliefs upon which their right to manage was founded.

As I spoke to growing numbers of executives about productivity, quality, and U.S. versus Japanese management, I became increasingly convinced that a new statement of beliefs about management's role in the American corporation was needed.

My own discussions with executives about their management began to change. When I asked them about their own values, and about the values that they wished to see instilled in their firms, I found they were giving a great deal of thought to the culture of their corporations and to the cultures that would be required in the future. Out of these sessions I was able to start defining the values of the future corporate culture.

There is a new corporate culture emerging in American business. The decline of the old business culture and the struggle to establish a new one can be observed in almost every major corporation in America. Its motive forces are the financial necessity of improved productivity and quality and the demands made by employees for a more satisfying work environment. But new cultures are not built upon material necessity alone, they result from the creation and acceptance of new values, new visions, a new spirit. New cultures emerge when leaders proclaim and demonstrate those values through their own behavior.

This book examines the new values, visions, and spirit that are arising in the American corporation. It is not concerned merely with the techniques of the new management, it is concerned with its soul.

The current anxiety about the American corporation and its productivity has resulted in a furious investigation of management techniques. Experimentation has never been greater, and it is clearly the result of the new economics of world competition. However, while this experimentation is healthy and encouraging, it is focused primarily on technique or structure. New techniques or structures succeed because they are an expression of an accepted value or spirit. The Catholic Church represented the creation of a new organization, a new structure. It could not have evolved in the absence of the spirit of Christianity that was its motivating force. Any explanation of its creation that ignores the values upon which it was built is inadequate. This motivating spirit created a willingness to sacrifice personal well-being for a higher purpose, a vision of the future. The American government as a structure similarly did not emerge simply because a technician perceived that the separation of powers, checks and balances, and representative democratic process were superior to other preceding forms of government. On the contrary, there was again a new ideal, a new vision of the future, a new spirit, articulated in the Declaration of Independence. The soul of a new nation was born.

There are values and a spirit at the foundation of how we organize and manage our corporations. These values are the deeply held beliefs, often unarticulated, that are the product of the culture's conditioning, its heroes, myths, and fears. These beliefs have emerged over the course of our nation's development, silent partners in the management of America's business. The answer to improved productivity, the remotivation of the business corporation, will not be found in simple management techniques. It will be found in the acceptance of and action upon new values. What is lacking is an examination of the soul and spirit of management, the foundation upon which management's right to manage rests.

The acceptance of new values has the power to create new cultures. Western culture has its roots in the Judeo-Christian tradition. American culture was created by the values of freedom of speech, religion, and the press. The culture of American commerce was founded on the ideas of free enterprise, free trade, and the novel notion that any individual could, with wit and work, attain wealth. The Marxist idea of the distribution of wealth according to need was sufficiently powerful, albeit flawed, to create revolutions. Thus, simple ideas can possess enormous power—the power to create a new society and to achieve a new standard of living. They can be the catalyst for the release of human potential. If we are to create new cultures within our corporations, we must determine upon which values we will build those cultures.

We take values for granted. The managers of our corporations are largely unaware of the cultural forces upon which their actions are based and cannot therefore question or alter those forces. How many managers understand the cultural roots of the command leadership that they habitually practice? How many realize they are operating in blind obedience to the conditioning of years of movies and television that proclaimed models that led to victory in ages now past? These managers act on assumptions that are likely to be of little benefit to the corporation of the future. What are the values, the spirit of management upon which the future corporation must be built? What are the values that will promote competitive success in the new world in which the corporation must compete on a global scale?

I have identified eight primary values which I believe will lay the foundation for a new competitive American corporate culture. These values are not borrowed from another country in the hopes that their implantation here will duplicate foreign success. We are too good for that. The American culture is too strong, too unique, too deep; it has been and will continue to be a model for the rest of the world. The competitive spirit is strong and well in American business, and it is this spirit that will propel us toward change. To compete is to seek a better way, to change, and it is what we do best.

The eight values are labeled "primary values" because they are applicable to the management of all organizations, and indeed many successful companies are already acting on them. I have selected these eight because my colleagues and I have observed they are the ones most related to high innovation, loyalty, and productivity. In brief, here they are:

THE PURPOSE PRINCIPLE

We all have a need to confirm our self-worth. Self-worth cannot be achieved in the absence of a sense of contribution to some higher purpose. Leaders fulfill this need. They communicate purpose to those who follow. The ability to communicate a valued purpose is a rare art among corporate managers. Achieving return on equity does not, as a goal, mobilize the most noble forces in our souls. The most successful companies have defined their aims in terms of product or service and benefits to customers in a manner that can inspire and motivate their employees. Most corporations do serve a worthy purpose. Individuals seek to identify with it. The competitive leader will make the connection between our souls and our work, and will benefit from the energies released.

THE EXCELLENCE PRINCIPLE

Our culture values comfort, both material and psychological. We feel we should achieve personal satisfaction and fulfillment. We not only value this comfort, but feel that it is our due. We do not welcome personal tests and trials, we seek to avoid them and view them as contrary to satisfaction. Satisfaction and excellence are inherently in conflict. Satisfaction implies acceptance of things as they are. Dissatisfaction is the source of motivation. It leads to actions to change that which is the source of discomfort. The achievement of excellence can occur only if the organization promotes a culture of creative dissatisfaction.

THE CONSENSUS PRINCIPLE

Managers are stuck in the culture of command. They feel an excitement, an exhilaration when they are able to command. Unfortunately, command behavior is what was successful in the crisis climate of battle The leader of old marched ahead of his troops because he was the strongest and the most brave. He exemplified the values that were important to that organization. The future corporation will not march into battle. It will succeed by its ability to bring ideas together, to stimulate the employees and managers to think creatively. The employee will not be asked to risk life and limb for his superior. He will be asked to risk sharing his thoughts and feelings. He will be asked to focus not his physical energies, but his mental energies. This change in task necessitates a change from command to consensus.

THE UNITY PRINCIPLE

Our corporations maintain the traditions of a class society. We maintain the distinctions of management-labor, salary-hourly wage; exempt-nonexempt, thinker-doer. They are all false distinctions, the old, useless baggage of a deceased society, carried forward into a new world. We live in an age of unity, of integration, when distinctions that disunite and limit people are inherently counterproductive. There are other traditions from our past to which management must return. There was a time when ownership and identity with the job were a source of pride. The industrial age, with the anonymity of mass production, swung the pendulum from ownership to alienation. The electronic age, with its emphasis on information, the flexibility of information technologies, and the psychological needs for community, identify, and a source of personal worth, will swing the pendulum back toward ownership. The competitive corporation will accept the value of fully involving the individual in its workings and decision making so that he or she again feels in unity with and ownership for his work.

THE PERFORMANCE PRINCIPLE

In Western society the corporation is the agency that metes out more rewards and punishments than any other. The prevalent principle by which it distributes its rewards is power. Those who organize, those who are in short supply, those who can control have power and are rewarded in proportion to that power. The distribution of rewards according to power is as old as our civilization. However, this system contains within itself the seeds of its own destruction. When rewards are granted without regard to performance, productivity suffers. When they are tied to performance, individual and corporate performances improve. If the corporation is to succeed in the new era we are entering, it must reevaluate the values by which it distributes its rewards. In the future rewards must be granted according to the value of performance, a value not currently exhibited at the level of the chief executive or the union apprentice.

THE EMPIRICISM PRINCIPLE

We are not skilled thinkers. Much of the explanation for the poor performance of American industry in recent years can be found in the sloppy mental habits at every level of our organizations. It is a myth that American managers manage by the numbers. Most of them have little understanding of data, statistical methods, the use of empirical analysis. However, this is only a reflection of the larger culture. We are a nation of sloppy thinkers. In the school, in the supermarket, and in the executive suite we make decisions based on gut reactions that are often easily manipulated. Intuition is most useful when it is founded on a sound knowledge of the facts. Intuition in the corporate culture is more often an excuse for lazy and undisciplined analysis. If we are going to improve our corporate performance, we must begin to teach the value of statistics and their appropriate use at all levels of the corporation.

THE INTIMACY PRINCIPLE

The military model of management was necessarily impersonal. In battle the cost of personal involvement in the psychological world of another individual presented too great a risk to the emotional well-being of the leader. This is our tradition. Strength is represented as a detached, masculine absence of emotion and intimacy with fellow human beings. Management style will inevitably change because the future corporation is faced with a different challenge. The new challenge will be to tap not the physical labor of the individual, but his inner thoughts, his emotional and spiritual energies. This will require an intimate culture. Tasks will be accomplished when individuals are able to share openly without risk of emotional punishment, when managers have intimate knowledge of their subordinates' thoughts, feelings, and needs. But intimacy requires a strength and security that are not promoted in most American corporate cultures.

THE INTEGRITY PRINCIPLE

Decision making in our organizations has become dominated by a concern for legalisms, regulations, and precedents. Integrity is the foundation upon which must be built all other values, and upon which rest the trust and relationship between individual and corporation. The ability to discriminate between what is honest and what lacks honesty is a skill that is critical to the establishment of the new corporate culture. We live in a society of law and legalism in which the lawyer has become the corporate high priest of right and wrong. That which is honest has become confused with that which is permissible by law. Our managers and corporations generally adhere to what is legal. However, the law does not specify what is right, and it is a poor guide to making the decisions that will establish trust and unity between individuals and organizations, between customers and suppliers. These relationships have deteriorated to the point where they represent a drag not only on productivity within major corporations but also on their ability to market their products in this country. When managers are able to discern and act on that which is honest in spirit, trustful business relationships will be reestablished.

The American corporation is not dearly loved by the populace. The corporation is viewed as an impersonal edifice of materialism. It neither inspires man to achieve his highest aspirations nor inspires the loyalty and devotion that would contribute to its own purpose. American managers have a tradition of pragmatism which is a traditional source of strength. However, this pragmatism may require the balance of new values that are lofty, that do inspire the imagination, engage the loyalty and devotion of the common man.

I share the concern expressed by Michael Novak in *The Spirit of Democratic Capitalism* that Marxism, despite its record of failure to provide material well-being, has succeeded in capturing the imagination and dedication of masses of people. It has done so precisely because it is uninhibited in its expression of lofty ideals and principles. American capitalism has failed to win the imagination and devotion of the world's population, and it has succeeded in eliciting the worst emotions from a large mass of the population. This is not entirely the result of the rhetoric of Marxism. It also arises out of a failure to define and express our purpose in terms that are inspirational. Ideas must be expressed in ways that appeal to the individual and that allow him to feel that he is dedicating himself to a noble purpose, that his efforts have meaning, and that he is contributing to the building of a future of which he can be proud. This is the foundation of motivation.

The search for meaning and significance is a central characteristic of the human soul. Every person would like to find meaning and significance in his or her work. How many corporations provide this opportunity? The degree to which an organization is perceived to be in pursuit of and is acting consistent with noble ideals is the degree to which it is possible for the individual to believe that his or her efforts on behalf of that organization will be personally meaningful and significant. It is this spiritual deficiency in the culture of our corporations that we must address.

It is my hope that this book will assist managers to examine the values of their own corporations. I am not so foolish as to assert that the values proposed are the "right" values. However, I am confident they will contribute to effectiveness within the corporation and to meaning and satisfaction for the individual. I will have succeeded in my purpose if managers are stimulated to examine the values upon which they are acting and those which they will need to incorporate in the future.

The book is organized into two parts. Part I presents the eight primary values, those that I consider to be applicable to all organizations in the new era we are entering. Part II presents a model for creating strategic and tactical changes to build the new corporate culture. I had not intended to make this a "how to" book. Initially it was my intent merely to present the principles for a new corporate culture. However, among the helpful feedback that I received from a number of readers whose judgment I respect was that the principles left one asking, "OK, I accept the principles, so what do I do to make all this happen in my company?" Part II is designed to provide a general guide to implementing culture change in the corporate setting. Chapters 10 and 11 concern themselves with strategy, defining the current and desired cultures and the forces of influence that impact the cultures today and tomorrow. Chapter 10 discusses a number of the more secondary cultural values, those which may vary depending on the business and its environment, and suggests guide-lines for deciding upon those as well as upon the primary values. Chapters 12 and 13 provide some basic tactics, some of the lessons that I and my colleagues have learned through numerous efforts to improve the culture of client organizations.

Throughout the chapters of this book I have called upon examples from our experiences with dozens of fine clients, including some of America's most successful corporations. Primary among these companies are Continental Group, Honeywell, Inc., Xerox, Exxon Corporation, American Express, Delmarva Power and R. J. Reynolds Tobacco Company. I owe a sincere debt of gratitude to the executives of these companies and to many others who have provided proof that American executives are forging a new corporate culture based upon values that will inspire the confidence and dedication of future generations.

PART ONE

PRIMARY VALUES

The following chapters attempt to describe the changes occurring in the culture of the American corporation, provide a very brief history of the transitions through which management has already passed, and suggest the need for new values. I then propose eight primary values, those that will evolve as common cultural assumptions of the American corporation. Most readers are likely to disagree with the selection of at least one of the eight. Some may not forgive me for failing to include another, or will otherwise question my judgment if not stability. Agreement concerns me little. The result I desire is that the values and assumptions by which we manage be actively debated by those who bear responsibility for our corporations' cultures and, thereby, the production of our nation's wealth.

ONE

Management's New Era

It is now the task of every corporation to examine its own culture, not merely for the sake of its competitive position, although that should be reason enough, but because it is the culture of our business corporations that will determine the future wealth of our nation.

We were meeting at the University Club in Milwaukee sixteen months after the change effort had begun. There were Steve, the division general manager; Hank, his director of manufacturing, to whom seven plant managers reported; two of those plant managers; the corporate productivity director; and myself, assisting in the effort to create a change in the culture through employee involvement. We were at a crossroads in this effort. We were there to address one of the conflicts that inevitably result as a culture shifts. Three of the seven plant managers had volunteered to participate in the program. They were very enthusiastic about attempting to involve the employees in decision making. They shared feedback on performance with all employees daily, met with all employees in weekly team meetings, and increased the use of positive reinforcement. One of the plant managers, the first to engage in the effort, brought graphs of his plant's productivity over the last three years. For the past year, during which he had been using the new techniques, his productivity had soared over that of prior years. There was no doubt that the program was achieving measurable results and was being greeted enthusiastically by most of the managers and employees involved.

Steve was around forty-five years old. He had been with the company for about twenty years, the normal tenure in this firm, which was in a mature if not declining industry. Steve was sincere in his desire to involve employees. He had called this meeting because I

had written a letter to the executive vice-president in which I outlined the strengths and weaknesses of the program to date, and the
changes that would have to be made if there was to be a lasting
difference in the culture. The executive V.P. had circulated the letter to his division heads. Steve wasn't too thrilled when he read it.
He felt that he had supported the effort, he had heard good reports
and believed it was going well. My letter presented a less comforting
picture.

There were few problems in the plants themselves. They were
anxious to adopt the program, they saw the results and bought in
enthusiastically. The problem was that the division managers had
changed little. They didn't know what to do differently, they hadn't
participated in the training, and the plant managers, with their increased awareness of what actually motivates people, were becoming
disgruntled with the autocratic behavior of their bosses. My letter
had outlined the problem of division managers lagging behind in the
change effort; they were acting as the "keepers of the culture," not
leaders in moving it forward toward a more creative and productive
environment. The culture of this company was strongly influenced
by many years of combat with the steelworkers' union and by the
reduction in business over the past five years. A third of the plants
had been closed, promotions frozen, salaries held in check. They had
not been fun places to work.

Now that the change effort was moving forward well in the
plants, the division managers would have to begin to change their
own behavior. If they didn't, the effort would become just one more
in a long series of management initiatives that came and went, each
well intentioned and each leaving little in its wake. My letter suggested that behavior consistent with the new style of management
would have to become a criterion for promotion, job assignment, and
bonus determination. The executive V.P. had written "Right!" in
the margin next to this paragraph before he had the letter copied and
circulated it. This was getting serious. Now the division managers
wanted to know what they were supposed to do.

Steve, the division general manager, leaned forward and asked me
to outline what I thought should be done at the division level. He
was comfortable, knowing that he could adapt to the new culture.
He liked people. He knew how to listen. He trusted and was trusted
in return. He watched Hank sitting to his right. Hank kept his arms

folded through most of the morning, leaning back away from the table, saying little.' Hank was sixty years old, a stern old warrior; he knew how to run a manufacturing operation and never could understand why others didn't. One of the plant managers had told me that in fifteen years they could not recall Hank praising them for any achievement. You were supposed to do a good job and in Hank's world, there was little reason to praise people for things they were supposed to do anyway. Hank was not comfortable with this meeting, he resented my letter, he resented me, who had never run a plant, who was I to be instructing him, the old veteran? He had a point. I could not have run one of his plants. I knew nothing of their equipment or manufacturing process.

I explained what division managers could do to strengthen and encourage the change effort. They needed to go through the training themselves so they could help their plant managers. They should be consulting with the plant managers, giving them advice on their management style. They could have division-level problem-solving teams to work on division-wide problems. However, these were the easy things. The difficult part was closer to home. Each of them had to struggle with his own management style, with his willingness to listen to the managers in the plants, with his ability to praise them for their good performance, with his willingness to trust his subordinates. Each had to believe it. Each had to practice it.

Hank, his stern face tightly controlled, his lips twitching as he listened, was reaching the limit of his control. Finally it came out. "You misled us! You did a pretty poor job of marketing this program. We never understood that this was for division managers. I've been managing these plants for more than thirty years and I don't intend to go around buttering up hourly employees. They know their jobs and I know mine. I listen to my plant managers. If they have any complaints, let's hear 'em. They know when they're doing a good job, too. They don't need me patting them on the fanny!" Steve was watching Hank, and when he finished Steve slowly turned his head toward me with a pained, almost ashamed smile. Steve suggested we go on to the next item of business. He didn't want to respond to Hank's outburst; neither did I.

You could easily get angry at Hank. He is tough and unsympathetic. He is the antithesis of the participative, new-era manager. He is, on one level, the problem. However, Hank is also the victim. He is a cultural casualty, conditioned by a system that required managers to be tough and unrelenting. He fought the unions and was rewarded for his toughness. He drove his managers hard and got results. He was rewarded again.

Hank is in pain. Intellectually he acknowledges what is going on in his company and in so many others is right. Emotionally he is uncertain of his ability to adjust. He is being asked to make a leap from combat to cooperation and is afraid of the fall. His pain is one of betrayal and he is right. He has been betrayed. He was taught to be tough and commanding. Now he is being asked to be sensitive and encourage participation at every level. He is the casualty of the future shock that is sweeping now through our corporations. And he is not alone. He is in the good company of the majority of America's managers.

AMERICAN CHALLENGE

American management is under challenge. "Everywhere, American products and American know-how are being challenged, even in product lines in which U.S. superiority has long been taken for granted. More and more, the competition is coming from rivals as big and well financed as the U.S. giants."[1] The American corporation has been bombarded with news of its failures and accosted for its inability to arise to the new competition. "But the golden age of growth is over. The U.S. standard of living is shrinking . . . the American credo that each generation can look forward to a more comfortable life than its predecessor has been shattered."[2] The era we are entering will require new organizations, new behavior, and a new spirit. The future will be characterized by global competition, and those corporations that will succeed will be ones that adopt a corporate culture with values that promote the behavior of competitive success.

SEASONS OF MANAGEMENT PAST

Of all my college professors, Dr. Barton was certainly the most memorable. He taught a course in Western Civilization. He loved it. He taught us to love it. He would lean on his podium and breathe into the microphone as he went through his slides, which he had prepared for every lesson, encompassing the total history of mankind. True, he gave us merely an overview of history, but of those parts of history that are worthy of remembrance. We would go through centuries and civilizations in weeks. We learned that civilizations had come and gone before, and that we were not unique. He taught us to see the patterns so that we could achieve perspective.

Spring, Summer, Autumn and Winter—twenty-one civilizations have passed through those four stages. Most of these civilizations are known only for their ruins that lie under jungle vines and exist under layers of building and decay beneath European cities. Once great and now gone, there were patterns in their rise and fall, and Dr. Barton set out to convince us that the cycles were repeating themselves and that we could make some sense out of history and today. As he flashed his slides on the screen, he would outline the conditions in late Rome, the arenas filled with citizens screaming for their favorite gladiators, and among his slides he would quickly show one of the Dallas Cowboys without comment or he would mumble something like "How did that get in there?" He would portray the decadence of late Rome and Greece, the obsession with personal pleasure, the orgies, and again there would appear "accidentally" a slide of The Den, a local beer joint where college students hung out. His lectures were so relevant and enjoyable that it was normal for five to ten unenrolled students to be sitting in the back of the room, there to be entertained.

Oswald Spengler and Arnold Toynbee, the great German and British historians, believed there were recognizable cycles to the rise and fall of civilizations. Long after Dr. Barton's course I actually read parts of Toynbee's twelve-volume *A Study of History*,[3] in which he documents the patterns of civilizations. If these patterns do exist, they have relevance today. They offer evidence that the changes in management style presently being pursued in America's corporations are not just another fad, but represent an adaptation to a new era, a new civilization building on the confusion of the old. A validation of the dual process is apparent; the old order is declining and a new one is taking its place.

The early days of a civilization, the Spring, are characterized by a people, simple, perhaps barbaric, lacking sophistication, complex institutions, or culture. They are, however, dedicated. They have a new religion, a new cause, or a great leader, a Mohammed, an Alexander, for whom they are willing to fight and die. They have a simple energy. Their spiritual life is dominant. They are not confused about their purpose or their mission. They know the purpose of their lives: to further their religion, to die for their leader; and because their lives are never comfortable or filled with great expectations for personal fulfillment, they will follow. They will obey.

The leader leads literally—in action and in spirit. He rides his horse in front of the army, he is the first to charge. He is among the strongest, fastest, and bravest. He acts out the values of the people who follow him, and the honor he receives testifies to the virtue of those actions. By his actions he inspires dedication and sacrifice among his people. His spirit inspires the spiritual life of his community. The management task is simple and clear.

Because of their focused energy, the people do succeed and they conquer. Their territory expands, there are new people to rule who are not from the same tribe, language, or loyalties. They have new problems. Somehow they must administer these new subjects. Conquering would have no meaning if they were to allow their subjects to rule themselves. They must impose their superior culture, values, and systems upon the conquered. Someone will have to specialize in this, someone will have to teach the values, religion, language of the conquerors.

As the once-simple people succeed in conquering, they take on a new set of problems to which they must adjust. They have supply problems. The military is growing in size and complexity and now someone must specialize in making armor, spears, and wagons to haul food. Someone must organize people to produce, and someone must procure the raw materials, and someone must distribute that which is produced. Specialization and management become recognized pursuits. Now there is a need for a different kind of leadership. Just as the military leader was the idealized warrior, the leader of wagon makers is the one who is the best craftsman.

The Summer of a civilization witnesses the development of the institutions of specialization. Specialization results in efficiency and greater success; more specialization, more complexity and changes in motivation and purpose. Now one may be motivated, not to die for The Cause, but to become a successful and recognized builder of wheels, trader, or teacher. Institutions of learning emerge to train people in the increasingly complex specialties. Libraries are built. Technologies develop. The citizens and leaders recognize they are a great power, a great civilization, a great culture. By every measure they are a success.

The quality of life has improved substantially. There is less hunger and fewer die as a result of war or disease. Life is becoming more comfortable. Expectations are on the rise, and the citizens expect their institutions to provide increasing levels of safety, comfort, and pleasure. They do, and expectations rise again.

The Autumn of a civilization sees a great transformation in personal motivation. The spirit of the people is changing. The religion or leader who was once the primary source of motivation in the Spring now is secondary in people's lives. Personal success is defined by one's relationship to society's institutions and the acquisition of personal wealth. The force of this motivation helps to build the institutions. People want more education so that they can have a better chance of succeeding, and the need for education grows with the increasing complexity of the institutions and technology. Students remain in school longer, require more professors, more buildings; the great university emerges with all its trappings of scholarship and ritual. Managers are motivated to climb the ladder of organization, and they recognize this motivation in their subordinates. The organization grows, positions are created to fulfill not only the genuine needs of growth, but the personal needs of managers who continually require promotion. The ladder is extended, positions are created upward and sideways, driven by the desire for personal success, so well ingrained in the citizens' children.

It is working. The entire system of personal motivation, institutional growth, development, and increasing sophistication is producing more wealth, more comfort, freeing people from drudgery and long hours. Leisure time has increased entertainment, and athletics are now significant interests of large numbers of people. The arts flourish and the civilization has truly produced a culture in all its forms. The manager has become the most important player in these institutions. He achieves his goals by the system of rewards that the institutions provide. There is little that appeals to a higher cause or spirit; there is no call to sacrifice one's self to the good of the larger group or for a divine purpose. Now it is promotion and pay.

During the Autumn of a civilization the institutions of commerce, politics, education, and religion play primary roles in everyone's lives. They are seen as the source of success and the cause of each failure. The demands on these institutions and the managers who must make them productive grow with an apparently never-ending escalation of expectations. But this is a cycle that must inevitably reach a point of corruption and conflict.

The achievement of comfort is the very cause of a society's failure. The citizens have grown to love their good life, their leisure, their comforts, their diversions. They have mastered the art of achieving rewards. They have come a long way from the primitive willingness to fight and die for a simple cause. The citizens now have little interest in serving in the legions that once were honored and now are garrisoned in some primitive outskirts of the conquered territories. Not only is there little motivation for this type of service, but success and comfort have become so commonplace that they are expected to be achieved with less and less expenditure of labor on the part of the individual.[4]

The Winter of a civilization is the period of crisis. All institutions are thrown into turmoil as a result of the changes in man's motive forces. The family, once the bedrock institution of the culture, is itself open to question. In late Rome it was common for a citizen to have as many as eight marriages, each based on convenience and financial and political connections.[5] The church becomes impotent. The government, looked to for resolution of conflicts and for preserving the pattern of ever-rising standards of living, becomes the source of frustration, is despised and increasingly unstable. The rascals are thrown out with growing frequency as they fail to solve problems that are beyond their control if not comprehension.

Individual motivation is in crisis. The pursuit of pleasure takes on a greater intensity as a blanket over the emptiness of purposeless lives. The orgies of the Roman citizens, the consumption of drugs, alcohol, and the abandonment of sexual restrictions and loyalties have all been characteristics of the Winter of many civilizations. The people are hard to govern now; they are educated and demand to know all the answers, they challenge all decisions and are convinced of their right to their comforts. Stagnation in productivity, inflation, and economic crisis were common ingredients of the approaching end of each once-great civilization. The people had gained education and sophistication, but had lost their collective soul and with it the energy that had made them great.

THE CHALLENGE OF THE NEW ERA

If we accept the lessons of history without reservation, we may conclude that we are doomed. Civilizations, one after another, have emerged and subsequently vanished, and we appear headed on the same course. However, this is not the lesson. An age is ending and a new era beginning. Old ways will not work and new ones must be found. We cannot assume American supremacy in technology, strength, or influence. But will our society be swept away by the new barbarians? No.

This is an age of world integration, not disintegration. The new era will be one of unity, global communications, and competition. We now have a world whose parts are so interdependent that the destruction of just one part would represent a loss for the whole. While the example of the decline and fall of the Roman Empire is usually given to imply that there was a victor and a vanquished, the truth more closely resembles a situation in which integration with a larger world replaced the narrower culture and opportunities of the old civilization.[6] Surely, we too are entering a new era and a new civilization, global, interdependent, intercompetitive, and ever advancing.

And what are the challenges presented to American management in this new era? I believe the following transitions will change the role of management:

1. Motivation by material reward alone is becoming increasingly inadequate. Personal needs are less material and more spiritual. The successful manager will respond to the needs of the spirit. The manager must learn to create a new productive spirit within the enterprise. The manager's job must be to assist his employees in the achievement of their own self-esteem.

2. The nature of work is less physical, more cognitive. In the past it was undesirable for workers to think creative thoughts. They were required to do repetitive physical jobs that were best done in the

absence of thought. These jobs are rapidly disappearing. The task of management now is to cause people to think creatively, to learn, and to share. The management of creative thoughts is best accomplished in a participative and positive manner. It is impossible to command another to think creatively. A management style that elicits high-quality thought is essential.

3. Individuals have options that they did not have at one time. Our old management style is based on the assumption of narrow choices. The worker labored in the local mill or he didn't work. Workers now have broad options. They can move, retrain, organize. Successful management must recognize the availability of options and the reality that management is competing with those options for the services of the worker. It is for this reason that management through intimidation is dead and management by involvement and positive reinforcement is just beginning.

4. The number of managers will decline substantially. The "knowledge worker" (even factory workers are now knowledge workers) requires fewer supervisors if he or she is properly trained, involved, committed, and rewarded. Those managers who remain will be skilled technicians who will consult with and assist their subordinates, and they will be practiced in the art of obtaining commitment rather than commanding.

5. We are entering a world economy. Worldwide competition will be not only for technology but for management competence. We are now being challenged, not because other countries have developed greater technology but because they have challenged us in management skills. Managerial competence will be the most critical determinant of corporate and national success in the new competition.

Mobilizing the energies of the workers of today and tomorrow will require a new set of beliefs about the nature of work, workers, and the task of management. In working with our major corporations, I have found that developing the specific skills of listening, problem solving, and reinforcement is not terribly difficult. The more difficult task is ensuring that these skills will be used. If these skills are at variance with the manager's beliefs and values, they will not be used. If they support the values of the manager, they will be used. We must begin to alter the basic definition of the management task, create a different set of expectations, beliefs, and values about what a manager does and how he influences others. The old ones have proved insufficient. If our organizations are to survive, they must take on not only new forms and structures, but a new productive spirit.

TWO

The Purpose Principle

The distinction between the leader and the manager can be summarized by the word "purpose." Leaders have a noble vision of their purpose. Leaders create energy by instilling purpose in others.

The chilling winds of a New York winter provided little comfort as I approached the glass edifice that housed one of the world's most successful financial institutions. I was not entirely sure that my report would not be met by a response more piercing than the winds accelerating through the canyons of lower Manhattan. My finding seemed almost too simple and perhaps too challenging to the leadership of the chairman of the company. The revolving doors brought relief from the cold. And as I signed in with the stern-faced guard who was far too serious about his duties, I imagined my departure following a failed meeting, being refused permission to leave, trapped for discovering the wrong answer.

The chairman had been concerned about the turnover among the senior executives. The firm was a headhunter's paradise. There was a general lack of esprit de corps and loyalty among the very best and most successful managers. I interviewed the twenty-five senior executives. I suspect that their average annual compensation was in the $200,000 range. They ran a worldwide multibillion-dollar organization that was held in very high esteem. I pursued my usual line of questions in interviewing, the ones that had always proved fruitful before: "If you could change one thing about the way that you are managed, what would it be?"; or "What do you like best about working for. . . ?" I also asked specific questions about objective setting, review of performance, feedback, recognition, rewards, decision making, etc. The more questions I asked, the more I became convinced that these managers managed each other very well. They understood the basics of good management technique and practiced them. They were very intelligent and hardworking. Throughout all my questioning only one consistent complaint was voiced.

These executives were not sure what business they were in. They were unsure of their purpose. Yes, they understood very well that they were in the business of financial services, and that they were excellent at providing them. But recently their firm had made several acquisitions that had nothing to do with financial services. Why? What was the plan? How would this affect their careers? Was the ladder to the top through the well-established financial services, or would it be through these new ventures? The truth is that no one had the answers to these questions. The acquisitions had been made because the parent firm had a lot of cash, saw the opportunity to acquire high-growth, high-potential profit companies and improve their return on assets. These were financial decisions made by financial managers. However, the managers below them, who might very well have made the same decisions if they had been in a position to do so, experienced the acquisitions in quite a different way. These new ventures upset their cosmos. The managers had now lost that consolidated sense of business and social purpose that had served as a primary source of motivation.

The senior executives felt no great loyalty to this firm despite its success and prestige and the rewards it had bestowed upon them. The executives were highly trained and skilled, and they were in demand. They would be well paid and would obtain positions that satisfied their essential needs here or elsewhere. It was something else they wanted, and—perhaps because all their other needs were so well met—they knew what it was. It was a sense of mission. They wanted to know what they were working for. What was the strategy? where was the firm headed and why? and what were their roles in that strategy? Their inability to understand the mission of the corporation and their roles in the fulfillment of it was a source of substantial dissatisfaction.

My encounter with the chairman increased my respect for him. He listened to my explanation thoughtfully and understood. He agreed. He felt it himself. His sincere desire to do what was best for the business and for his fellow executives was his dominant motive, and he took pleasure in considering the alternatives. When I departed, the guard had changed. He was a she. Young and attractive this time, almost flirtatious. As I left the building I noticed that the wind had ceased its attack.

A THEORY OF THE BUSINESS

How can such a successful corporation lose its sense of purpose? This firm is by no means the worst offender. It has become common in our age of conglomerate corporate politics in which movement up the *Fortune* 500 ladder appears to be of greater significance than providing quality goods and services. The devotion to product or service has become less prevalent than the devotion to financial success. The mystery is that the devotion to the former is most likely to produce the latter, while devotion to financial success is less likely to produce either. We can blame the business schools and consulting firms who have promoted a type of strategic planning that mistakes financial manipulation for the more noble activity of creating wealth. Many of our corporations' executives do not understand the difference between the organization and the consolidation of wealth and the creation of wealth. Mergers and acquisitions give rise to a new organization of wealth, one firm now having greater assets than before; however, no new wealth has been created in the process.

Peter Drucker has been writing about the importance of business purpose for many years. Perhaps the idea is too simple for this age of complex analysis. "Every one of the great business builders we know of—from the Medici and the founders of the Bank of England down to IBM's Thomas Watson in our day—had a definite idea, had, indeed, a clear theory of the business which informed his actions and decisions. A clear, simple, and penetrating theory of the business rather than intuition characterizes the truly successful entrepreneur, the man who not just amasses a large fortune but builds an organization that can endure and grow long after he is gone."[1] A "theory of the business," as Drucker refers to it; or "superordinate goals," as Richard T. Pascale and Anthony G. Athos discuss in *The Art of Japanese Management*;[2] or a basic philosophy or beliefs, as Thomas Watson, Sr., so successfully instilled within IBM. Tom Watson, Jr., clearly credited IBM's success to these beliefs: "I firmly believe that any organization, in order to survive and achieve success, must have a sound set of beliefs. Next I believe that the most important factor in corporate success is faithful adherence to those beliefs."[3]

Unfortunately, many of our most senior corporation executives have only the most shallow understanding of the purpose of their businesses. Too many of them will tell you that this purpose is to maximize return to stockholders. This says nothing at all. It is indicative of a manager who has been trained in technical skills but has no loyalties, no loves, and no business of his own. To maximize return on investments, assets, or profits is an inadequate statement of purpose. It is inadequate for two reasons: First, it completely fails to accomplish the paramount responsibility of leadership—to provide meaning and inspiration to those who are expected to follow. Those who do the work of the corporation must focus their energies on either product or customers. They must be motivated toward producing or creating the best possible product, or providing the best possible response to the needs of their customers. It is the responsibility of the executive to motivate employees toward this purpose. They are not and should not be focused on "return on assets." This result will follow if employees focus on that which they can influence and in which they can find personal meaning and reward.

Second, financial objectives are an inadequate statement of purpose because they fail to recognize the social justification for the existence of the corporation. This justification is a creative one. The purpose of the corporation is the creation of wealth, those goods and services that enhance our standards of living. When the corporation increases its productivity, it produces more goods and services at lower cost and thereby increases that which is available for consumption. This is an increase in the aggregate wealth of society. When the corporation produces a new technology or reduces the cost of technology, such as was done with the microcomputer, again it makes available a higher standard of living.

The creation of genuine wealth, goods, and services for consumers must be the primary purpose of the corporation. Achieving financial results is necessary, but secondary in purpose. Financial results will follow as the corporation and its stockholders succeed in their primary aim. To focus on financial results first detracts from the firm's ability to achieve those results because it fails to mobilize human energy.

Wealth is not money. Wealth is that which may be bought with money. Throughout the world there are many economies producing more money and less wealth. They are faced with this dilemma precisely because their productive institutions are inadequate to fulfill the primary purpose of producing the goods and services that comprise true wealth. The government can produce money; it does not produce wealth. This is the social purpose, the noble purpose, of our business institutions.

Robert B. Reich has articulated the problem deriving from the inadequacies of purpose and the failure to distinguish between the creation of wealth and its reorganization: "Managers have indeed adapted by innovating. But innovations have not been technological or institutional. Rather, they have been based on accounting, tax avoidance, financial management, mergers, acquisitions, and litigation. They have been innovations on paper. Gradually, over the past fifteen years, America's professional managers have become paper entrepreneurs."[4] "The problem is that paper entrepreneurialism is supplanting product entrepreneurialism as the most dynamic and innovative business in the American economy. Paper entrepreneurialism provides nothing of tangible use. For an economy to maintain its health, entrepreneurial rewards should flow primarily to products, not to paper."[5]

Andrew Carnegie understood the difference between the creation of genuine wealth and the manipulation of finances. In his later years, when he formed the Carnegie Steel Company, he pursued a very deliberate policy of creating a more productive enterprise while avoiding the financial manipulations that were very much the common practice of the day. His success was largely attributable to his devotion to the business of making steel rather than to reorganizing the symbols of wealth, stocks, bonds, and legal documents. A congressional committee later described his battle with the steel trusts as "a contest between fabricators of steel and fabricators of securities; between makers of billets and makers of bonds." Carnegie described one of the competing steel trusts as "the greatest concern the world ever saw for manufacturing stock certificates . . . But, they will fail sadly in steel."[6] He was right, they did! While his competitors focused their energies on the manipulation of wealth's symbols, Carnegie devoted his attention to making steel at the lowest cost. Carnegie built not only one of the nation's largest and productive enterprises, but one of the largest fortunes of the day which later he dedicated almost entirely to philanthropy.

LEADERS VERSUS MANAGERS

America has too many managers and not enough leaders. If we had more leaders we could do without half of the managers. The distinction between the leader and the manager can be summarized by the word "purpose." Leaders create energy by instilling purpose. Managers control and direct energy. Leaders define success in terms of the accomplishment of a business achievement, the success of a product or service. Managers define success according to measures that are derived from the process of business independent of the content of the business. Leaders appeal to the higher values, the long-term potential of the individual to feel a part of, a contributor to achievements of mankind. The manager appeals to the immediate needs for income, status, and security. Leadership brings out the creativity of the individual and inspires courage. Management without leadership produces conformity.

Our civilizations were built on the vision, the inspiration, the spirit of a religious leader. Western civilization emerged driven by the spirit of Christ. The Islamic civilization was founded and flourished because of the inspiration of Mohammed. So, too, have many of our major business organizations come into being, driven by the vision and the spirit of their founders. General Electric eventually emerged as a result of the creative genius and inventiveness of Thomas Edison. The Ford Motor Company emerged from Henry Ford's deep belief that there was a need and a mass market for cheap and dependable transportation. His mission was to create a manufacturing process that would make this transportation available at an affordable price. Such visions instill an energy not only in the individual entrepreneur who creates them, but also in those who follow in pursuit of the visions.

At this point in history, it is not the norm for individuals to find fulfillment of a higher purpose through their work. However, it is also not the norm to be highly dedicated and energized by work. If asked why they work, few would answer that they are fulfilling a mission. However, when asked, most will acknowledge that they would like to feel that they are accomplishing a purpose, a social good through their work.

A few years ago I was working with a manufacturer of metal products.[7] The culture of this company was in crisis. It had been very successful and was still successful. It had become a large conglomerate, with the metal business now representing only one of several businesses. The Boston Consulting Group had been hired by the corporation to assist in strategic planning. The metal company met the criteria for a "cash cow" almost perfectly, and the corporation followed the prescribed scenario of taking cash out of the metal company and buying higher-growth, potentially more profitable businesses. Money was not put back into the company for technical development, new equipment, or expenditures on the development of people. At the same time, overcapacity in the industry resulted in price erosion and subsequent plant closings. The company was not helped by its highly adversarial relationship with its unions. The managers were fine examples of a macho style of authoritarian management; they were uncreative and fearful for their jobs, and they intimidated their subordinates.

I was leading a one-day self-assessment session with a group of about twenty middle-level managers in this metal company. After giving the managers a model for assessing their culture, I asked them to form into small groups for about forty-five minutes to define some characteristics of their firm that they found attractive and some that they would like to change. Each of the four or five small groups nominated someone to report to the larger group the characteristics they had identified. When the last reporter spoke, he presented his impressions of the culture in a way that must not have been the result of the group's consensus.

"I remember ten or fifteen years ago, I used to work twelve hours every day, usually six days and sometimes seven days a week. I remember how I couldn't wait until I got to work in the morning. I would have done anything for this company. We were 'The Metal Company,' and we were proud of it. We were the best and we knew it. Now it's different. Now I come to work and I do my job because I'm a professional. But it is no secret that there are people at the top of this company who are ashamed of the word 'metal.' Now you have to search through the annual report to find it. We all know that they have no interest in this business except for the money they can drain out of it. Now all I hear people talking about is how long they have to go until they retire." He stopped, and everyone knew he had tears in his eyes. There was a long, quiet pause and he was not contradicted.

PRODUCTS, PEOPLE, AND CUSTOMERS

Purpose comes in many forms. It need not be the salvation of mankind. Being "The Metal Company," the best in the industry, is purpose enough for most people. Many managers and employees working in the personal computer business believe that they are the vanguard of a new day that will see our lives radically changed by easy access to computer technology. This is their purpose. Once, I visited a meat-packing plant that made sausages. I listened in awe as the manager of the plant explained to me how more people in the South woke up each morning to eat that company's brand of sausages than any other kind. He actually described for me his conviction that the quality of their sausages helped all those people enjoy the rest of the day. He truly believed it. He believed that the work he was doing was for a noble purpose. He was helping millions of people have a good day! All of these managers and workers are motivated by their own thoughts. They think about the good they are doing, the pride in being the best, the satisfaction of leading a change in life-style or making the best sausages in the world. They have purpose, and this purpose leads to productivity and satisfaction.

During recent decades there has arisen a cadre of executives at the top of our corporations who have served more to destroy purpose than to create it. These antileaders have put together some of the largest conglomerates in the nation. They have done so not by building a business but by the organization of finances. Many of them have never made an item, delivered a service, or sold a product to an actual customer. They know numbers. They do not know products, services, or customers. Success to them is found solely in the numbers. They have increased the size of their fiefdoms while understanding nothing of the businesses within them or of the motivations and fears of their employees. The managers who must run the businesses within these fiefdoms understand that they are judged now only on financial criteria, not on the merits of advancing the state of a technology, producing the highest-quality goods, or being respected by customers. These criteria are meaningful only to someone who loves and cares for the business of making clothes, fasteners, or furniture. If a manager's energies are directed more on the resulting numbers and less on the business itself, the business deteriorates. This scenario has been repeated a hundred times during the past decade.

The executives of our corporations did not go to leadership school. They went to management school. I recently spoke to a group of students at the Wharton Business School. Afterward, I chatted with four students who were obviously job hunting. I asked them, by the time they graduated with their MBAs, how many courses in managing, motivating, or leading people would they have had? They agreed without apology that the right answer was NONE! When they spoke about business they spoke about strategic planning models and quantitative theory. These students left me with the impression that they knew everything about numbers, models, and theoretic strategy but nothing about the substance of business or what business managers actually spend their time doing. They were prepared to enter the world of number manipulation. But when I asked them what type of business they would like to be in, they agreed that it didn't matter as long as it was one of growth potential. When I asked whether they were interested more in sales management or manufacturing management, they reacted with some disdain. They had no interest in these activities, they were interested in finance and strategic planning. They were not interested in spending time where actual business is conducted—in producing and selling—they wanted to ascend immediately to the high post of condescension, planning strategically in complete ignorance of the business.

This total deemphasis on the management of product, people, and customers in our supposedly best business schools is one of the most frightening facts of American education. Leading large groups of people and resources without a purpose more significant than that derived from playing a game of Monopoly is only one part of the problem of the way we are producing technical and financial managers.

Business strategy follows from a business purpose. If our business purpose is "to make available information processing and management technology to every home in America," then strategies of technical research, product development, marketing, and manufacturing must follow, and they can follow only from an understanding of and enthusiasm for the business purpose. None will follow a purely financial objective of increasing return on equity. The purely financial objective causes one to make decisions that lead away from a coordinated business purpose. This is not to say that financial objectives are undesirable. Of course, a business must achieve financial objectives, and these can motivate and direct performance constructively. However, those monetary goals should not be the primary motive forces in the creation of a business; they are a secondary method of measuring one aspect of its success.

THE SEED OF MOTIVATION

Understanding that the business serves a higher purpose not only results in sound and creative strategy, it also results in the willingness of individuals to sacrifice. We will sacrifice, in our personal lives and in our businesses, if we have a valued vision of the future. I remember listening to managers at Honeywell's Aerospace and Defense Group talk about the time when they were working on the Apollo program. They worked insanely long hours and with total dedication. They worked as if they were at war. They felt that they were responsible for landing a man on the moon and that this nation's pride and prestige were in their hands. They made personal sacrifices that no manager could ask or demand. They were not motivated by the financial aspects of their project. They were not responding to management techniques or evident self-interest. They were responding to what they felt was a noble purpose, and through sacrificing to that purpose they achieved self-esteem.

Our need to motivate through purpose, to lead, is not only present within our corporations. It exists as a dilemma of our democratic capitalist society. We believe that our system of democracy and capitalism is the vehicle for achieving the highest living standard and the highest order of individual and collective freedom ever attained by mankind. Yet this system is failing to inspire others. Masses of people, particularly in those parts of the world which most need the productive impetus, are inspired not by our system, which has proved successful, but by one that has repeatedly failed to produce wealth or freedom. Why? Because in those areas of the world, they speak of freedom and power for the peasants while we speak of investments and acquisitions. Talk of "freedom and power for the downtrodden people" does inspire action. Our talk of investments and acquisitions is without meaning. Why are *we* not the revolutionaries leading the poor to freedom and ownership of the means of production when we have more experience with freedom and the ownership of the means of production than any people on earth? Because we have forgotten how to lead. We have forgotten how to inspire. We are consumed by our knowledge and love of techniques when knowledge and techniques have little meaning for those who need inspiration and will respond only to a higher purpose.

We who are the leaders of the institutions of free enterprise have a nearly sacred responsibility to make a connection between the effectiveness of those institutions and the human soul. "Throughout the world, capitalism evokes hatred. The word is associated with selfishness, exploitation, inequality, imperialism, war. Even at home, within the United States, a shrewd observer cannot fail to note a relatively low morale among business executives, workers, and publicists. Democratic capitalism seems to have lost its spirit. To invoke loyalty to it because it brings prosperity seems to some merely materialistic. The Achilles' heel of democratic capitalism is that for two centuries now it has appealed so little to the human spirit."[8] The financially oriented are satisfied with the proof of financial success. Unfortunately, the mass of people, within our society or within our corporations, are not primarily motivated by what is rational. It is the emotional—the appeal to the self-esteem, the spirit—that is the prime mover.

We must learn to create and utilize purpose in the management of our business and our nation. Business enterprises do have a noble purpose and we should recognize and proclaim it. The purpose of business is the creation of wealth—not for a few, but for all. Wealth is not money. It is the goods and services that business provides. It is we who are able to produce wealth who will eliminate poverty, disease, and ultimately war, who will free humanity from the chains of mindless toil so that we can pursue and utilize our higher capacities of mind and soul. Peter Drucker made a similar observation a number of years ago: "The achievement of business management enables us today to promise—perhaps prematurely (and certainly rashly)—the abolition of the grinding poverty that has been mankind's lot through the ages. It is largely the achievement of business management that advanced societies today can afford mass higher education. Business both produces the economic means to support this expensive undertaking and offers the jobs in which knowledge can become productive and can be paid for. That we today consider it a social flaw and an imperfection of society for people to be fixed in their opportunities and jobs by class and birth—where only yesterday this was the natural and apparently inescapable condition of mankind—is a result of our economic performance, that is, of the performance of business management. In a world that is politically increasingly fragmented and obsessed by nationalism, business management is one of the very few institutions capable of transcending national boundaries."[9]

Each business in our society, whether making steel, farming potatoes, producing cars, or processing information, each in its own way contributes to this collective purpose. We who have the opportunity to choose must meditate on our purpose, communicate it to our managers and workers so that they may have the satisfaction of sacrificing their energies toward that which enhances their own dignity. This is the first priority of business leadership in the new age.

THREE

The Consensus Principle

The successful manager of the future will make full use of the collective wisdom of those within his jurisdiction and he will learn to derive pleasure, not from the making of decisions, but from assuring that the best possible decision is made.

They were mere specks on the horizon. Three sails, one now growing slightly larger than the others. For months the men on the British frigate had waited for the French to make a move, and now from the direction of shore, "Two frigates, one ship of the line, triple decker, sir," came the yell from the man on the top yardarm. Hornblower said nothing. He paced back and forth on the sternmost part of the poop deck. They knew not to disturb him. Even Bush, who had served with him for ten years, knew that nothing except the most unthinkable news could be cause to disturb his captain when he was in this state. The months of boredom had been filled with the anticipation of this very moment. Hornblower had been waiting for an opportunity for action, but now he felt betrayed. He was hopelessly outgunned. He knew that as many as half his men would be bloodied casualties by the time the sun set that day. He would likely spend the rest of the war rotting in a French prison, unless, of course, he was buried at sea. He felt only hopelessness.

"Lieutenant Bush. Ask the officers to dine and perhaps some tea." "Aye, aye, sir." Bush turned away in puzzled obedience. Hornblower had made a practice of inviting his officers to dine before battle. It would be four hours before they would be engaged, plenty of time for food and conversation. But now all of the men on the ship knew that this afternoon they would see battle. They had no choice. They were there to prevent the French escape, and the Admiralty in London would have no interest in the advantages or disadvantages of a blockading ship. The officers had faith that Hornblower, or perhaps the myth created by the stories circulated in the officers' club in London, would devise a plan that would allow them to sleep peacefully once more. Hornblower had no such faith.

Over dinner Hornblower called upon all of his energies to be calm and even entertaining. His men smiled, amazed at their captain's ability to ignore the impending doom, and struggled to enjoy themselves. Hornblower was only partially with them. On some deep and hidden level his mind was racing to consider the possibilities. Then he felt it. The ship's attitude changed slightly. Yes, the wind was backing. It would turn now toward the shore. Suddenly there was a plan. If the rumors were correct, his frigate had five degrees' advantage close-hauled to the French ships of the line. They would have to beat off the shore. He dismissed his men and they filed out of the room as if departing for the last time.

Hornblower stood now on the poop deck facing the wind. He surveyed the apparent chaos below him as the men ran fore and aft, clearing the decks for action. Hornblower would wait until the French were within range before bringing the ship to the wind. His officers stood below in silent obedience, none knowing the actions they would be required to take within minutes. "Mr. Bush. Gunports open." And now Hornblower heard the rumbling sound of seventy-six guns being rolled out from the gunports in perfect unison, and he felt the confidence of knowing that the months of endless drills had prepared his men for their duty. The sound of their earnest feet upon the deck assured him of their obedience.

THE CONDITIONING OF COMMAND

Ah yes! The thrill to command. That was leadership. Hundreds of men responding in disciplined order. A leader who could make decisions and had the confidence to command. And if they disobeyed they would be court-martialed and hung. Yes, indeed. That's when men were men.

Every red-blooded American male can imagine, can feel that thrill of command. It is deep within our souls, this knowledge of true leadership. And we know it is within us. We are each confident that it is only due to the accidents of history that it is not we who are standing there on the poop deck, in command, giving orders in the face of battle. This is our conditioning, the training of our culture.

Horatio Hornblower never gathered his lieutenants together before battle and asked, "Now tell me, do any of you fellows have any ideas. . . ?" Nor, while they sat in a circle, did he ask, "How do you men feel about. . . ?" Real men don't sit around in circles asking questions. Real men command!

Horatio Hornblower is the hero of C. S. Forester's novels and is modeled after Lord Nelson, Britain's greatest naval hero. On one level these novels are mere adventure stories. On another, they are a thorough documentary on the development of the leadership qualities of the stereotypical British naval captain. We cannot look back on these qualities and say that they were wrong. They worked. They won the day.

Many historians feel that the British Empire at its height represented the high point of Western civilization and that it has been downhill since. The institution that enabled Britain to rule two thirds of the planet was its navy. And the key to the success of the British navy was the quality of its leadership, the skill and character of its ships' captains. The lessons of Hornblower are a study in the management skills that guided what may be one of our civilization's most successful institutions. Hornblower's style of management was successful, it was right, it worked. And it was entirely different from that which we are asking of our managers today.

Hornblower gave orders and would never ask his subordinates for advice. If he overheard an idea from one of his officers that he wished to use, he would never give credit to that officer. He did everything to hide his weaknesses and appear omnipotent. He could and did demand absolute obedience from his men.

THE REQUIREMENTS OF COMPLEXITY

Why are we now asking managers to behave in totally contrary ways? Not because of the Japanese. Not because of Theory X, Y, or Z. We are changing our management style from command to consensus because the managers at General Mills never have the opportunity to pull broadside to broadside with the managers from Pillsbury, open their gunports, and start firing. They may wish they could. At the end of the day they would know whether they had won or lost. They would at least know if they were heroes or fools. Now they receive no such satisfaction. The competition in products, markets, and technology is complex, requires high interdependence, and occurs over a long time period. The management task has completely changed, but we have not. The manager cannot demand blind discipline of the men on the lower gundecks and flog those who move too slowly.

We are changing our management style because the material realities, the actual nature of the task, have changed dramatically from the days of Hornblower and Nelson. Then, for their task, command won the day. Today, for our task, command will prove as disastrous as consensus decision making would have been aboard the H.M.S. *Victory* at the Battle of Trafalgar.

In days past it could honestly be said that the commander had all the knowledge available to him with which to make decisions. His subordinates had no additional information. There was room for only one person to think and make decisions aboard a ship of war. The men, who were pressed into service, usually drunk and oblivious, were slave labor. Blind obedience was all that was required of them. Today virtually all workers, even factory workers, have more education and training than did the officers of the British ships of war. Today few jobs do not require thought and self-initiated action. No manager in any position of significant responsibility in our corporations can possibly have all of the knowledge and experience with which to make decisions. The functioning of a business is too complicated and competitive. The input of all members of the organization is needed. No slave labor exists in any business today. Our workers have more options than did the lords and ladies of Britain in her prime.

We are moving from command to consensus leadership because the material realities of the work in which we are engaged are changing. Theories can only attempt to explain what is already happening.

Unfortunately, the future is moving upon us so rapidly that we are all cultural misfits. When I tell the story of Horatio Hornblower to groups of managers, and particularly when I get to the point about hanging men for disobedience and I say, "This is when men were men and they didn't sit around in circles. . . ," the audience often applauds, or at least smiles enthusiastically. They are reacting from the gut. They are releasing the tension of conflict between the old culture in which we are conditioned and the new to which we are all trying to adapt. These emotional responses are within us. They are part of our culture and particularly so for males, who have received all of the male stereotyped command conditioning society provides. What our emotions tell us is right, what feels good are unfortunately maladaptive and the remnants of a life that is no more. Our corporations are inhabited by misfits, struggling to sort out the responses they were taught would work but now do not.

There is a survival-of-the-fittest selection process at work. Two hundred years ago it selected the British naval captain. Now it will select for survival whoever adopts those management practices that are workable for an organization that relies on the management of thoughts, voluntarily contributed and created. The authoritarian commanding manager of the past will become the dinosaur of tomorrow. The workers whom organizations rely on for present-day complex tasks cannot be commanded. They must be led through positive leadership. They have too many options. The manager is competing for their services, not by pay alone, but with the human environment that he creates and with the opportunity for personal satisfaction. Only by creating a culture of involvement, and by deriving satisfaction from the creation of consensus, will the manager win this battle and feel the exhilaration that Hornblower felt as he turned his frigate into the wind.

The culture of the American corporation continues to act on the assumed value of command leadership. Managers place a high value on the ability of the manager to make decisions himself, quickly. Allan Cox conducted a comprehensive survey of middle managers and executives in a sample group of U.S. corporations.[1] He concluded that "approximately 70 percent of executives report that their corporations strongly or somewhat encourage both speedy decision making and a high energy level and fast pace on the job." Seventy-three percent of top executives reported that their companies valued quick decision-making ability; and 67 percent of middle-level managers reported the same value.

The entire world is moving slowly toward consensus decisions. In days past, the leaders of nations were free to command. Today they are driven by the pressures of the world community toward consensus. When the United States invaded Grenada, Ronald Reagan made a decision based on consultation with a few other Caribbean nations, but not with the consensus of Great Britain or other countries. Much of the debate following this act centered not on whether it was the best decision for the people of Grenada, but rather on whether the President of the United States should make consensus decisions with his European allies or whether he should decide on his own to take military action.

CONSENSUS, CONSULTATION, AND COMMAND

Consensus is the process of human interaction that results in a course of action. It is the product of frank and honest discussion by all parties, to which all are willing to commit themselves as if the decision were their own. The consensus process involves the person who must carry out a decision in the creation of that decision. In so doing, the individual feels ownership and commitment to the decision and to his group. As a result of consensus, the participants understand why action is being taken and the considerations that went into the decision. They can explain it to others.

Consensus decisions represent the sum of all the knowledge and experience of the group. Because consensus decisions are generally complex and long range, they are best arrived at by a careful consideration of the accumulated knowledge of many people. Better, more creative decisions result and more determined, united action follows. The management task of today requires the development of a consensus process, and our leading corporations are rapidly recognizing and acting on this need.

Managers learn to be people of action. They learn that those who succeed and accomplish are able to act quickly and decisively. Managers almost universally have an aversion to sitting in meetings or submitting to "management by committee." This bias is well justified, based as it is on sound experience in the real world, and it leads to an almost assured objection to consensus or participative management. Therefore, this justified bias toward action *and* the need to develop consensus—a process necessarily requiring delay—must be rationalized. The answer is to clarify which decisions are appropriate for consensus and which require other means.

It may be helpful to break decision making down into three categories, command, consultative, and consensus:

Command decisions are those the individual manager makes without discussion with his subordinates or team members.

Consultative decisions are those the manager makes but only after discussion, either one-on-one or in a group, with other managers or persons who have knowledge or interests related to the decisions.

Consensus decisions are those the manager turns over to a group of his peers or subordinates, and which are made after full and frank deliberation by the group and to which all agree to adhere as if the decisions were their own.

I have asked groups of managers to keep a log of all the decisions they make during the course of a week. Then I have asked them to indicate whether they feel those decisions should be command, consultative, or consensus. Then I have asked them to present their decisions to their teams. Typically, some common patterns emerge and the group can agree on principles by which they will make decisions in the future.

Command decisions tend to be very short-term operating decisions or crisis decisions. The majority of command decisions happen so quickly and are of such a detailed nature that managers are often not even aware that they are making them. For example, a manager's secretary walks into his office and asks, "When you visit Denver next week, which clients did you want me to arrange appointments with?" He responds by rattling off the names of four clients whom he has wanted to visit or his local salesman has suggested he should visit. He gives little thought to this decision. It is one of dozens he will make this day. This is typical of an appropriate command decision. His subordinates or peers would think he was crazy if he consumed their time with such decisions.

The other types of command decisions that are appropriate tend to be those which occur very infrequently, during a crisis. Fire, theft, equipment breakdown, illness, or other events may trigger a crisis that requires immediate action. No one will disagree that these are appropriate command decisions and are as near to the battle-command scenario as most managers will ever get.

Managers spend more time making *consultative decisions* than any other type. These decisions tend to be of moderate significance.

They usually require some investigation, some consideration of their impact on others in the organization, and perhaps some internal selling. These are the decisions that are often made by two or three individuals in an informal setting, by the coffeepot or in the hall. Again, in most of these cases it would be a waste of time for an entire management team to meet to consider them.

Consensus decisions, those that should be dealt with by the group, are those with strategic implications: To produce a new product or not. To open new sales territories. To bring a new partner into a small law firm. To make any change in the direction of the organization that will impact the majority of its members. These decisions are in the minority, and most managers will agree, in principle at least, that they should be made by consensus. Getting the managers to do so is quite another matter.

We don't like to make consensus decisions. They are a pain in the neck. Sincerely turning a decision over to a group of peers or subordinates requires that the manager put his trust in the group. This is not part of his training. He has learned to trust himself, to rely on his own survival instincts.

CULTURAL MYTHS OF INDIVIDUALISM

We have all been conditioned by the television set. We have grown up watching a series of stereotypical roles played out before us. And these years of watching TV have taken their toll. Today's generation of managers have learned values and behavior of which they are hardly aware. They grew up watching *The Lone Ranger* or its clones. The programs all followed the same pattern. There were always the "helpless victims." These were usually an elderly rancher and his unmarried granddaughter, who lived with him. They were going to lose the deed to their ranch, the railroad was going to run through their house, or their cattle were being rustled. The plots never varied. The victims always got themselves into this fix, but never, never could they get themselves out of it. These characters were among the dumbest creatures ever placed on this planet.

One of the interesting characteristics of *The Lone Ranger* was that there was always a "problem" of "exciting" magnitude, and it was always solved within a thirty-minute period. It was never unsolvable

and it was never just partially solved. At the end of the show the bad guys were behind bars.

Problems were always solved the same way. The Lone Ranger and his faithful Indian companion (read servant of somewhat darker complexion and lesser intelligence) come riding into town. The Lone Ranger, with his mask and mysterious identity, background, and life-style, never becomes intimate with those whom he will help. His power is partly in his mystique. Within ten minutes the Lone Ranger has understood the problem, identified who the bad guys are, and has set out to catch them. He quickly outwits the bad guys, draws his gun, and has them behind bars. And then there was always that wonderful scene at the end. The helpless victims are standing in front of their ranch or in the town square marveling at how wonderful it is now that they have been saved, you hear hoof-beats, then the *William Tell Overture*, and one person turns to another and asks, "But who was that masked man?" And the other replies, "Why, that was the Lone Ranger!" We see Silver rear up and with a hearty "Hi-yo Silver," the Lone Ranger and his companion ride away.

It was wonderful. Truth, justice, and the American Way protected once again.

Vicarious conditioning is the process of learning that occurs through observation. This is why we are rightly concerned about what our children (future managers all) watch on television. When behavior occurs on television and someone is positively reinforced (rewarded) for that behavior, the individual watching may be vicariously reinforced also. Behavior that is reinforced occurs more often later on. Surely vicarious reinforcement was taking place as the *William Tell Overture* concluded another story about the preservation of the American Way. We can still feel the rush of excitement as that deep voice proclaimed, "And with a hearty hi-yo Silver . . ." You can bet we were learning all through the thousands of sequences of *The Lone Ranger* we watched, we who are now managing this nation's corporations.

What did we learn from this cultural hero? Among the lessons that are now acted out daily by managers are the following:

• There is always a problem down on the ranch (read plant, division sales office, etc.) and someone is responsible.

• Those who got themselves into the difficulty are incapable of getting themselves out of it. "I'll have to go down or send someone down to fix it."

• In order to have the mystical powers needed to solve problems, you must stay behind the mask. Don't let the ordinary folks get too close to you or your powers may be lost.

• Problems get solved within discrete periodic time units and we have every right to expect them to be solved decisively.

These myths are no laughing matter. Anyone who has lived within or close to our corporations knows that these myths are powerful forces in daily life. Unfortunately, none of them bears much resemblance to the real world. The truth is more like the following:

• There is not always a problem down on the ranch. Just as often there is no problem until the senior manager appears on the scene determined to find one. In doing so, he often creates the problem. Managers are very poor at discriminating between normal fluctuations in performance and genuine performance problems. There is rarely a "bad guy." More often the problems result from a series of decisions in which many people played a role. The responsibility is collective.

• People who get into difficulties can, in the majority of cases, get out of them. By doing so, they enhance their skills and confidence, and are less likely to get into similar situations in the future. Most problem solvers sent to help depart with their "silver bullets," leaving the local folks just as incapable as when they arrived. Problem solvers must involve the person or group that owns the problem in solving it, and leave them with the skills and confidence to solve their own difficulties and to make future decisions on their own.

• If managers took off their masks of anonymity, became intimate with the local folks, they would be more trusted, have freer access to information, would be recognized not for their false powers, but for their ability to draw out the real solutions from the local people who are going to have to deal with the problems on an ongoing basis.

• In the real world, solutions to problems don't come in clean thirty-minute, one-month, or one-year cycles as we would like. Problems get partially solved this month, somewhat more the next, and perhaps may require two years and four months to be solved completely. Not neat at all. Problems are also not black and white, solved or unsolved. Managers like to proclaim they have solved a problem. It feels good to believe that they are taken care of so we can go on to the next one. This is how we wish the world to be, but it isn't. Most so-called problems that managers spend their time trying to solve are in reality ongoing situations that must be addressed forever!

The Lone Ranger represents just one of many cultural stereotypes and conditioning influences that inhibit our ability to adopt a consensus-decision-making model. We have no cultural heroes who made consensus decisions. Never did any of our heroes gather troubled people together and listen to them; ask probing questions to draw out the best within each; ask them to define the problem; suggest alternative explanations and solutions; and require them to reach a joint and unified decision. Can you picture this scene? The group facilitator stands up after the members of the group have reached a mutual decision, and they all turn toward the facilitator and applaud as the theme music is heard. You'll never see it. We must find some way to market consensus decision making better. It needs more sex appeal.

Many of the current efforts directed at participative management or consensus decision making will not work. They will not work for a number of reasons. The most serious reason is that they are being initiated at the bottom of the organization when they are most needed at the top. Quality Control Circles or Employee Involvement Teams are desirable. I have been involved in implementing these group methods in numerous firms, and the most significant element in their success is the degree to which senior managers begin to practice the same methods. If this type of problem solving becomes the cultural norm, it will last and be accepted by the organization. If it remains a "program," that is, culturally deviant behavior, it will die the death that every other management gimmick program has and should die.

I was recently invited to a steel mill in Youngstown, Ohio, by the president of the local steelworkers union. This steel mill, with about one thousand employees, had been involved in Quality Control Circles for about three years. They had forty-two active circles. I met with the union president, his two Circle coordinators, who functioned in that role on a full-time basis, and two of his union stewards. The union president explained to me that he and his local supported employee involvement. They understood the need for productivity improvement and were willing to cooperate. That was the good news. The bad news, this union president reported, was that during the past three years management had not changed one bit. They still thrived on combat and authoritarianism. They not only found it difficult to cooperate with the union in making improvements, they didn't cooperate with each other.

The industrial relations manager, whose responsibility it is to deal with the union, told the union president that his goal was to maintain about four hundred grievances in process at all times! It was the union president's goal to have none! Hard to believe, but true. The union would soon confront the president of the steel company and insist that unless management began to change its own style, the union would no longer participate in any problem-solving activities.

This case is not unusual. There are many executives within American corporations who have a heavy investment in the adversarial relationships that have dominated dealings between union and management. The vice-president for human resources of a major manufacturer recently confided to me that the process of employee involvement which he himself had initiated and championed was very threatening personally. If it actually worked and eliminated the combative relationship between union and management, he would lose power. For years his job had been to be at the forefront of that combat. He was the hero in victories against the union. He knew how to conduct the battles and win. The very process of adversarial relations was his power base in the organization. If it was reduced, his power and prestige would be reduced. To his credit, however, he knew that the course of involvement, cooperative problem solving, and shared gain was the inevitable direction of the future, and he led in the development of these goals because he believed in their value.

The executives of our corporations are endorsing participative problem solving. However, they are more comfortable with this process on the plant floor, between supervisor and hourly employee, than in the middle and upper levels of management. This is typical of our approach to management practice. Delegate the location of the problem to a subordinate until it reaches the bottom echelons, when the truth is that the problem will not go away until those who are charged with leadership accept their responsibility of being in the forefront and serving as models of the new management. While programs may start as experiments in some isolated area of the company, if they are going to take hold and become a way of life, part of the new culture, senior executives will have to examine and change their own management practices. Their belief in consensus will have to be demonstrated by their deeds, not by their words alone.

FOUR

The Excellence Principle

Excellence is not an accomplishment. It is a spirit that
dominates the life and soul of a person or a corporation. It is the
never-ending process of learning that provides its own
satisfaction.

It was odd that two individuals could each hold the title of president
and be so totally different in skills, character, and outlook. I had to
perform the same task with each of them within the same week. I
was to give them my feedback on their strengths and weaknesses and
help them develop a personal self-improvement plan, the culmina-
tion of a long process of data gathering from them and their subordinates. On Tuesday I was to be in Chicago to meet with Bill
Harrison, the president of a medium-sized chain of men's apparel
stores in that area. On Thursday I would be in Minneapolis to confer with Jim Wilson, the president of one of Minneapolis's most respected corporations. (Both names are fictitious; the incidents are
not.)

These presentations were always somewhat difficult for both the
clients and me. They would receive the most blunt, uncensored, and
personal feedback they may have ever experienced. I took great pride
in being absolutely frank. While this made the service worthwhile to
them, it also created anxiety. There was always negative feedback,
some of which would come as a surprise.

I suppose that I should have been more concerned about my presentation to Jim Wilson. He was the more accomplished, intelligent,
influential, and important. He ran one of our nation's great companies. However, I looked forward to my presentation to Jim. It was
my session with Bill that was causing me most concern.

Bill Harrison had held the presidency of the retail chain for about
eighteen months. Before that he had been the number two man for a
similar company in the Southwest. He was young, about forty, had
a lot of energy, and was confident of his ability to succeed. Un-

fortunately, he was on a course to failure. Also I didn't feel that my feedback would be very helpful to him, because I didn't believe that he would really listen and digest the feedback. Bill had had few good models of executive ,behavior in his career. He possessed a *Playboy* magazine, made-for-television image of how an executive should behave. He played one subordinate against another. He did not tell his employees what he honestly felt about their performance. He had not established effective accountability, performance expectations, or direction for his organization. Bill was not respected. He didn't know what role to play. Worse yet, he thought he was doing a good job.

Jim Wilson could not have presented more of a contrast. As a respected scientist holding a doctorate, he had had a twenty-year career in high technology during which time he had a number of mentors who were well-respected executives. Jim had become a leader in the movement to humanize the workplace, involve employees in decision making, and improve productivity. His ethics and conduct were beyond question. When I interviewed Jim, he had no trouble identifying his strengths, but he was also painfully aware of a substantial list of weaknesses. He even questioned his ability to accomplish what his company needed. When I interviewed his subordinates, they all reported that he was a model of integrity, intelligence, and leadership. I did have negative feedback for him as well. They said he could be very authoritarian. Sometimes he became impatient with others who were not as quick as he was, and he didn't hide this well. This impatience could be very painful for subordinates who held him in such high esteem.

Presenting the feedback to both these presidents resulted in no surprises. Bill listened carefully. He was pained by the feedback, and I tried to help him digest it by putting emphasis on his potential as well as his deficiencies. I tried to be as specific as possible without betraying the confidentiality of the exercise. I tried to help him understand exactly what he could do differently in the future. However, he wouldn't commit himself to anything. He nodded as if he understood, but he didn't.

When I presented the feedback to Jim, the most difficult part was getting through the positive comments. He didn't want to hear them. He said, "Yeah, sure, I'm not interested in that," as I went down the list of the strongest qualities that his subordinates had identified. When I got to the negatives, he probed. He wanted to know exactly what was meant by "authoritarian." He wanted to know in what situations, with which level of people, and how could he have handled the situations differently? He was processing every bit of feedback with the intelligence that had apparently characterized his entire career. I learned later from people close to him that he was making deliberate efforts to improve in these areas and even acknowledging his faults in open sessions. His effort to address his own deficiencies served as a model again for others in the organization and increased their respect for him.

THE MECHANISMS OF EXCELLENCE

Excellence is not an accomplishment. It is a spirit that dominates the life and soul of a person or corporation. It is a never-ending process that provides its own satisfactions. Excellence results from an ability to learn, an ability to respond to one's environment in productive ways. Excellence is not one particular trait or another. It is, however, the product of a few psychological traits or habits that enable the individual to learn and progress. These habits tend to be shared within the culture of a corporation.

The difference between Bill and Jim was the difference between those who achieve excellence and those who delude themselves into the acceptance of their own mediocrity. They were both products and representatives of their corporate cultures. Bill had no significant models whom he held in high esteem and whom he strove to emulate. Nor did he have any high standards or values by which he judged himself. Because of the absence of such standards he was more easily satisfied with himself, and this satisfaction was in itself a cause of mediocrity. His motivation was to achieve the symbols of success, not to derive satisfaction from the process of self-improvement. Because he was more easily satisfied, he did not process feedback, he did not listen and learn. On the other hand, Jim had many models and mentors against whom he judged himself. He also possessed a set of values that he attributed to his father and his religion, both serving as sources of comparison. Jim was imbued with the energy of self-improvement. He listened and learned, he processed feedback. Jim was never satisfied, and his dissatisfaction with himself was the core reason for his accomplishments. He believed in his ability to control events. If things went poorly, he blamed himself and he took action to improve.

CREATIVE DISSATISFACTION

I have never met an excellent executive who was satisfied. I have met many mediocre executives who were. Those achieving excellence are participants in an ongoing struggle with their own competencies. They are active managers of their own learning processes.

Nowadays it is a strategic imperative that senior executives manage the culture of their organizations. One of the cultural traits they must instill is that of creative dissatisfaction. The most successful organizations have created a belief system in which it is assumed that the way things are done today will be inadequate tomorrow. They foster a pervasive spirit of excellence. Change is a continual expectation, a cultural norm. Change and progress occur as a response to dissatisfaction. If an individual is satisfied, then he or she stands still, has no reason to change, to grow, to become a closer approximation to his or her potential. Only out of dissatisfaction come searching, discovery, change, and growth. Individuals who possess this quality of creative discomfort are those who are in progress. They are the most valuable commodity of an organization in this age of transition. They are able to adjust to change, to benefit from it, and to lead change. The ones who are satisfied are the inertia, the drag on an organization.

It is the responsibility of the manager to create dissatisfaction among his subordinates. It is not the manager's job to cause his employees to be satisfied. No one performs to his maximum ability when he is satisfied. People do perform when they are dissatisfied. That dissatisfaction, however, must not be out of fear, since fear produces a controlling, stifling dissatisfaction. Fear may produce performance, but only in temporary conformity to someone else's instructions. Creative dissatisfaction, demanding more from oneself, results only from the knowledge that something better exists, from examples, and from anticipation of rewards.

Managers who succeed in creating a culture of excellence do so by constantly struggling to promote the three ingredients that result in excellence: standards, motivation, and feedback.

They establish standards, not necessarily formal measures but examples of excellence, reference points. They create heroes within the culture who represent a stereotype of what that organization regards as excellence. When people in a culture promoting excellence are asked to describe their ideal, they can point to individuals who have fought, suffered, and won. Some of their senior managers are usually among these heroes. They are confident that this idealized performance, this sacrifice will have its rewards within the organization. This establishment of standards has little to do with formal descriptions of desired performance, platitudinous statements written by the personnel department for senior executives to mouth. The standards must be real ones by which real people have lived.

Motivation is created by the process of objective setting, performance measurement, and rewards. Objective setting should not be a ritual, as it is in many companies. It should be a process involving all managers in the establishment of judgment points that are of consequence. Real measures are applied and real rewards are delivered to those who perform. It has been my experience when I have interviewed managers, that they have objectives that are set according to prescription each January, and that consist of a long list of twenty or thirty obviously desirable outcomes, which then are filed until next fall. If the managers are unable to verbalize their two, three, or four most important objectives without reference to a piece of paper, they are most likely having no impact on an individual's performance. When performance is outstanding, rewards are outstanding.

The habit of giving absolutely frank feedback is a condition necessary to the achievement of excellence. Feedback is the steering mechanism that points the motivated performance in the right direction. The healthiest organizations are those in which managers make a deliberate effort to give frequent and pinpointed feedback, and also promote the giving of feedback from subordinate to superior.

None of these practices will cause the individual to feel satisfied. They create a desire for something other than the existing condition. They create dissatisfaction, which leads to performance.

The need for dissatisfaction is not consistent with our popular culture in which feelings of discontent, discomfort, and guilt are taught to be indications of a neurotic personality. By modern standards of what constitutes a well-adjusted personality, the Apostles and geniuses of past ages would all have been viewed as neurotic and driven by obsessive-compulsive characteristics. God protect us from a society composed of psychologists' views of well-adjusted personalities!

Behavioral psychology explains behavior and performance as responses to reinforcement, the desirable consequences following a behavior. The history of reinforcement causes the behavior to occur more often. In order for reinforcement to work there must be a reinforcer, something the individual wants and will perform for. Money, food, approval, status, and security are all potential reinforcers. In order for a person to be motivated, reinforced, there must be some state of deprivation or absence. For example, if the individual has an unlimited supply of food the individual will not work for food because it is no longer a reinforcer. If people have as much food as they desire, they are satiated. Satiation occurs when an individual has a sufficient amount of something that he will no longer behave a certain way to achieve it. Satisfaction produces nonperformance.

Children in our culture are growing up with the notion that they have some inalienable right to achieve comfort or achieve satisfaction. Any denial of this satisfaction represents a defect in the structure of society rather than a failure in their performance. There could be no more dangerous notion. If we are to promote a culture of excellence, we must also promote the acceptance and validity of creative dissatisfaction. We must create the understanding that great accomplishments were achieved by great men because they set continually higher standards so as continually to challenge their already considerable abilities. They were spiritually alive! They never allowed themselves to become satisfied with conforming to standards that represented the mediocre norm. Unfortunately, we are now promoting a normative culture. In this culture, we do not measure ourselves against increasingly more challenging standards, but against the lowest common denominator, the normal distribution, and we find satisfaction in the fact that we fall somewhere above this denominator, never recognizing its pitifully low level and the destructive nature of the goal itself. This is the spiritual malaise of mediocrity, the illness that grows out of arrogance and complacency.

STANDARDS OF EXCELLENCE

The creation of standards of excellence, of models by which we compare ourselves, is critical to the achievement of excellence, and the absence of such standards is one of the explanations for our current passion for mediocrity. In an earlier day the average person and certainly the individual of achievement accepted a set of standards that were biblical in origin and were loosely termed "virtue." Benjamin Franklin devoted a section of his autobiography to "The Art of Virtue," in which he summarized the benefits of his lifelong program of moral self-improvement.

> To Industry and Frugality, he ascribes the early Easiness of his Circumstances, and Acquisition of his Fortune, with all that Knowledge which enabled him to be an useful Citizen, and obtain'd for him some Degree of Reputation among the Learned.

The virtues of industry, frugality, justice, mercy, temperance, and others were accepted as norms toward which mankind should strive and with which we would be compared on that day of judgment which, it was believed, we would all face. Excellence was defined by The Giver of the Highest Standards. Benjamin Franklin was not comparing himself with others and saying, "I am better than he, not quite as good as she, and surely, I am at least above the average." He had not entered into the downward spiral of comparison to norms that inevitably results in the rapid achievement of mediocrity.

With the growing dominance of organizations and the effort required to succeed within an organization, to climb the ladder, to be dependent upon the judgment of other people, the criteria for excellence and achievement increasingly became the image other mortals held of one. Self-help advice stressed less the comparison with ultimate virtue and more the ability to influence the view of the self held by associates. The ability to sell oneself to others became the key to success rather than the pursuit of inner virtue or substantive achievement. The emphasis shifted from accomplishing to influencing.

As standards shifted from absolute to relative, motives shifted, too: from the achievement of material rewards as a by-product of virtue to the direct pursuit of material rewards. This is exemplified by the advice of Napoleon Hill, one of the high priests of personal success in the recent past: "You can never have riches in great quantities unless you can work yourself into a white heat of desire for money." Ben Franklin, not an underachiever or one who failed to appreciate the good life, would have found this advice insulting if not sinful.

The current culture has seen a new shift, a move away from the crass materialism of Napoleon Hill, a rejection of the purely materialistic motive, and a rejection of the ability to win friends and influence people as a valid standard or motive. However, the current culture has not witnessed a return to the acceptance of the Protestant ethic, to Franklin's virtue. The biblical standards of virtue with their comforting credibility have not been accepted once more as the standards for personal self-worth.

What, then, are the standards of excellence with which our children, students, workers, and managers are to compare themselves? If not for heaven, for what final reward are they to be motivated to achieve the standards of our new era? It is beyond the scope of this book to attempt to prophesy the answer to this dilemma. Our society must eventually provide the answer if it is to rescue itself from a downward spiral of human effort. However, there are clear implications for those of us charged with establishing excellence within our organizations.

We have a responsibility to establish a culture in which there are standards of achievement, of human virtue that are exalted and openly and loudly proclaimed for all to hear. There must be heroes, acknowledged and praised by the organization for their achievement of excellence. We must ensure that every individual is challenged to meet progressively higher standards. We must put aside those systems of engineered standards that establish a uniform standard for acceptable performance. These systems institutionalize mediocrity rather than challenge one to strive toward even higher levels of performance. They necessarily establish a standard that is relative to the average performer, thereby failing to challenge the best and causing the worst to feel helpless. The new motivation must be as it is in athletics: to set progressively higher records, not to achieve a normative performance.

It is in this process of continual striving that virtue can be found, not in the meeting of a norm established by and for someone else. But it is the manager's responsibility to ensure that each and every individual is involved in such striving. This can be accomplished not only by the promotion of high standards of excellence, but by the demand for personal objectives and the most honest feedback to every individual.

THE LOCUS OF RESPONSIBILITY

There are lessons to be learned about excellence and achievement by observing those members of society who are at the other end of the spectrum. My first foray into the field of human motivation occurred when I was hired to serve as a counselor in Polk Youth Center, Department of Corrections, in Raleigh, North Carolina. I was the one and only counselor for three hundred and fifty young inmates. A couple of years later I was instituting a model behavior-modification program in another youth prison within the walls of Raleigh's Central Prison. The program involved the establishment of a free economy in which the inmates had to earn every privilege, including paying rent for their dormitory space, which included high- and low-rent districts. In this institution there were about one hundred and fifty inmates, aged eighteen to twenty-two. These young offenders had committed the more serious crimes. Thirty-three of the one hundred and fifty were in for murder. Others were in for rape, kidnapping, and armed robbery. They were a reasonably good sample of those not achieving excellence.

I believe I interviewed each of the inmates. And I did learn from them. What I learned had little resemblance to what I had found out about them when I read their files containing personal histories, including the description of their crimes. What I learned when I talked with them was that they didn't belong there. With almost universal consistency they reported a "reason" for their incarceration that had little to do with their own behavior. An inmate explained with perfect sincerity that he was there because the judge who sentenced him had also previously sentenced his brother, who looked very similar; the moment this inmate walked into the courtroom he knew he would be sentenced. Another explained with equal sincerity that he was in prison because his court-appointed lawyer wasn't really interested in helping him. The lawyer's lack of interest was the reason why this inmate found himself in prison.

Many of them reported the stories of their crimes, which usually involved the heavy influence of "the other guys." Their stories would sound something like this:

"I was on parole and had a midnight curfew. It was about eleven o'clock and I was sittin' in a bar, mindin' my own business. I was goin' to be home by curfew. Suddenly, these other guys I used to hang out with come into the bar. They say, 'Hey man, let's go for a ride. We got some wine in the car, man, let's go.' I told them I had to be home by curfew so I'd pass. They just grabbed me and pushed me into the car. So I'm ridin' around in the car, sittin' in the back-seat. Suddenly, the guy drivin' says, 'Hey man, there's this little gas station with this old man sittin' in there. He must have three hundred bucks sittin' in the cash register. We could be in there, knock the guy on the head, get the money, and be out of there in thirty seconds. There's no way anyone could ever catch us.' But I told him I didn't want no part of it. I told him I was tryin' to stay straight. But before I know what happened they pull up to that gas station, knock the old guy on the head, throw the money in the car, and those guys run into the woods, leavin' me sittin' there in the car with no keys. Up pull the cops and here I am."

Don't feel sorry for these young offenders. You can be sure that they were guilty. They were the "other guys." They were happy to accept responsibility for other crimes, those for which they had not been sentenced. I used to wonder what would happen to the crime rate if only we could have caught those mythological "other guys" who were responsible for all those young people being behind bars.

There is a process that psychologists have labeled "locus of control." This process explains the fact that we all have a tendency, somewhere on a continuum, to place responsibility for events in our lives either within ourselves (internality) or outside ourselves (externality). On the internality-externality continuum, prison inmates tend to be very external. They view events as being beyond their control. This is a psychological defense in that they need not feel so terrible about themselves if they do not see they are responsible for events. It is precisely for this reason that prison inmates are so difficult to rehabilitate. You aren't dealing with the responsible party!

When beginning to work with a new organization I will often interview the key managers of that organization. I will ask them to explain whatever performance deficiency they may be burdened by. The explanation will often reveal that the problem is "that damned union. All they want is . . ." Or, "If corporate staff would just keep off my back and let me . . ." Or, "If the economy weren't so . . ." The "other guys" are alive and well in American industry, presenting just as many difficulties as in the prisons of North Carolina. It is often hard to find the person who feels responsible for an organization's performance (unless of course it is good, in which case there is no problem at all).

The tendency of managers to place responsibility for events in their organization outside themselves, externality, is a cultural disease in corporations against which we must wage war. This displacement of responsibility is a force in direct contradiction to the achievement of excellence. Managers who achieve excellence respond to events in a highly internal manner. They see themselves in control of things, responsible for the way they are, good or bad.

When I visited the senior executive of a high-technology firm, the executive relayed to me his most recent concern. How he portrayed the concern was always similar. "Six months ago I put_____in to be manager of this division. I'm afraid he isn't going to work out. He just doesn't seem to be able to make decisions. Why did I do that? This is the second bad assignment like that I've made this year. I seem to be missing something when I make these high-level assignments. What's wrong with me?" In fact, there is very little wrong with this executive. He is one of the best I've ever met. But he believes in his own responsibility. He believes he can and should control events so that they turn out right. If they don't, it's not because someone else messed up, it's because he failed to judge the situation properly.

This manager is excellent because he is learning. The manager who views himself as responsible is constantly learning from his successes and failures. He is asking the question "What could I have done differently to have prevented that?" He will continue to refine his skills because of this process. This is the way to achieve excellence: the high standards for one's own performance, the setting of progressively higher objectives for oneself, and the acceptance of, even thirst for, feedback.

The best manager, and particularly the entrepreneur, may have an irrational belief in his or her ability to control the outcome of events. The purely rational manager would never have started Apple Computer, McDonald's, or dozens of other enterprises that are creative forces in our economic system. But heroes, those who accomplish great things against great odds, are never rational people. They are people with an irrational faith in their own ability, in an idea, in the system that allows them to accept responsibility and pursue their idea. If their judgments were entirely rational, they would rarely have chosen the course of action that resulted in their success. They are slightly "out of touch" in their belief in themselves and in their total disregard for the "other guys" who burden so many.

If our corporations and our nation are to compete in the coming era, we must deliberately promote the pervasive spirit of excellence. The creation of this spirit within the corporation is one of the most critical strategic tasks of management today. The corporation cannot instill within each individual the psychological mechanisms of excellence. However, it can promote an environment, a culture that reinforces and increases the probability that more of its members will become excellent.

The corporation and its managers can encourage an environment of intellectual inquiry in which the individual pursuit of knowledge becomes the norm. The manager can demand and reward individual objective setting, self-improvement, and initiative at every level of the organization. The manager can publicly recognize the heroes who sacrifice and achieve to the limits of their ability, whether they are scientists, secretaries, or factory workers. And the manager can design the systems and organization that cause individuals to feel that they can control their own destinies in a way that promotes the acceptance of responsibility.

FIVE

The Unity Principle

> The workers no longer want to be separated from
> responsibility. They want to participate in the business game
> and they want to play to win. Let's make them all managers,
> now!

We are all workers. We are all managers. It is time to create within
our organizations a oneness that is blocked by our adherence to the
traditions of a class society. We cling to historical divisions—
owner/manager/worker—that once facilitated growth and productive performance and now block them. It is time to replace this di-
visive class system in our corporations with a competency continuum
that recognizes that every employee must participate in management
and must perform productive work, from the factory worker to the
chief executive officer. The tradition that separates the manager and
the worker, the one assigned the thinking-deciding function, the
other assigned labor, is no longer consistent with the real-world demands of the modern corporation. The presumption that these class
distinctions are necessary to the running of an efficient organization
is a hoax. This hoax is perpetuated by the acceptance of tradition
and by the arguments of those in both management and labor whose
personal and political interests are threatened by the elimination of
the class system.

These divisions will be eliminated because maintaining them is
currently the greatest single barrier to productivity and economic
performance, particularly in the manufacturing sector. The false distinction between labor and management is the seed of labor discontent and management inefficiency. The worker knows now that he
or she is a "knowledge worker," even in the most basic of manufacturing industries. This worker is capable of self-management and is
rightly insulted when assigned the role of nonthinking, nonpar-
ticipating labor.

THE MYTH OF INFERIORITY

Much of the substance of American management is based on assumptions about labor that are erroneous. These false assumptions are expensive. They prevent us from utilizing the talents, abilities, and motivations that reside within the labor force. Becoming free of these myths will be among the keys to the effeective utilization of human resources in the decade ahead.

I recently completed an assignment to create an employee involvement process in a basic manufacturing plant in Omaha, Nebraska. The average tenure of the hourly employee in this plant was twenty-two years—twenty-two years of working on the same equipment in the same plant manufacturing the same product. There were forty managers and supervisors of two hundred and thirty hourly employees. The average tenure of the managers was twenty-four years, two more than that of the workers. How much advice and supervision can a manager who has worked at a simple manufacturing process for twenty-four years give to an employee who has worked on that same process for twenty-two years? Virtually none! In fact, most of the management and supervisory time was spent in one of two ways: first, in completing reports and gathering information for the next level of management; and second, in solving problems for hourly employees that should have been solved by those employees in the first place.

I remember my first day in this plant. I spent most of the day meeting with the managers, asking them to assess their management practices and culture. They were duly accepting of the corporate initiative to create employee involvement. I then met with the fifteen elected officers of the three different unions represented within the plant. When these esteemed veterans of labor trials filed into the meeting room, they presented a unified posture of silent strength and skepticism. Before I said my first words, three of them placed small tape recorders on the table and pushed the record button. I knew that I was on trial. The cooperation of these union veterans was essential to the success of the effort. They were holding their cards close to their vests.

I explained my views of the need to create a cooperative culture if the company was to survive, the need for all to change, from the company president on down. I detailed the process that we were going through, the implementation of team management at every level of the organization. After about fifteen minutes the president of the local International Brotherhood of Electrical Workers leaned forward, obviously prepared to render a judgment. "I'll tell you one damned thing," he said. "If you can get upper management to do this you've performed some kind of miracle. Fifteen years ago I tried to get something like this going but no one would listen to me. If you can get them to change you won't have any problem with us. We could save this company a ton of money if someone would listen to us." Everyone shook their heads and laughed in agreement. They knew that altering the habits of the old culture would be much more difficult for management than for labor. They were right. However, management did change and so did they. Gradually, managers and labor within the plant began to work in cooperative teams. Division and corporate managers began to alter their personal management style, becoming less critical and authoritarian and working more in teams. Over the next eighteen months, productivity as measured by "base board boxes of output divided by labor hours paid" increased 52 percent.

The current class system of management-labor, thinker-doer, creates work to justify the presence of excessive management; it denies the employee the opportunity to accept responsibility for his own work, adds to cost, and reduces performance.

Productivity and performance in our organizations will be improved as we create a spirit of unity between people at all levels. It is my experience that workers, possibly more than any other group, are prepared to accept new relationships and responsibilities. The workers no longer want to be separated from responsibility. They want to participate in the business game and they want to play to win. Let's make them all managers, now!

INTEGRATING MANAGEMENT AND WORK

Integrating management and labor was begun in earnest in many of our largest corporations. General Motors now has at least four plants in which much of the management between the plant manager and the work teams has been eliminated. TRW has a plant in Lawrence, Kansas, in which supervision has been eliminated; some managers have remained as advisers to self-managed work teams. M & M Mars opened a new plant recently in Waco, Texas, with self-managed work teams. Several other corporations are engaged in similar efforts. Each of these cases has proved highly successful with productivity and quality performance levels that surpass their prior performance or that of comparable plants.

The TRW Oilwell Cable Division plant in Lawrence, Kansas, is a good example of the benefits that can be gained when employees are fully involved in the management process. Gino T. Strippoli, General Manager, reported recently that "when the Oilwell Cable Division opened its plant in Lawrence, Kansas, in 1976, we wanted to avoid all the traditional bugaboos such as authoritarian policies, rigid work rules, and adversarial labor-management relationships that tend to inhibit an organization's effectiveness. The idea was to stimulate employee participation and spread authority by developing work teams that would serve in effect as the lowest level of management. The teams, all salaried, would be involved in such decisions as scheduling production, solving quality problems, evaluating performance, recommending equipment, taking disciplinary actions, hiring and training workers. The benefits of our program have been decidedly positive. Since 1978 we have achieved an eighty percent increase in productivity. Our absenteeism rate is about two percent; our employee turnover, one percent. Our profits after taxes and return on assets employed have increased by multiples. And we estimate that we need one third fewer employees to achieve the same output as a traditionally structured cable manufacturing plant would."

Strippoli offers a worthwhile insight into the obstacles to true employee participation. "There's one prerequisite: Managers must rid themselves of the illusion of total control. Total control, the frenetic, finger-in-the-pie approach, is neither possible nor desirable. Interestingly, our managers have found that by not striving for the futile ideal of total control, they gain more power in the best sense of the word—power as the ability to get things done!"

The new corporate leader will succeed by creating unity among persons in the organization and between the organization and its members. A spirit of oneness, harmony of purpose, common interests, and action will characterize the most successful organizations. All management practices will be aimed at the creation of this harmony. Individuals will be hired based on their ability to become an interrelated part of the culture of the organization. The systems of training and development will cause people to feel that the organization is their own and that they are interdependent parts of the whole. The systems of compensation and benefits will create an increasing mutuality of interest between each member of the organization. The concept of ownership will be expanded beyond our current definition of financial investment to include all forms of contribution to the enterprise.

THE PSYCHOLOGY OF OWNERSHIP

The unity between the individual and the organization can best be understood in terms of ownership. Ownership is a psychological condition, not merely a legal one. Ownership is the condition in which the individual feels that his or her own well-being is tied to that of the organization. It is the condition in which the individual is willing to sacrifice immediate self-gain for the good of the whole, in which the employee believes in the interdependency between the self and the organization. The individual will protect the organization from harm as he would protect his home, family, or community. When the psychology of ownership is present, the employee experiences pleasure if the firm succeeds and suffers pain if it fails. This is the unity we should be seeking.

I recently visited an assembly plant of the Ford Motor Company which was considering the initiation of an employee involvement effort. I conducted a series of interviews with the managers of the plant. The managers spoke very convincingly of their desire to create a greater spirit of cooperation with the union. This plant had a long history of fierce combat between management and labor, as the majority of this country's auto plants have experienced. After speaking with the managers, I spoke with the local United Auto Workers union president, Billie Joe Harris, whose deep Southern drawl and intensity left no doubts about his roots and affiliations. However, I have never forgotten how Billie Joe shocked me. I asked him what he hoped to see accomplished by any type of a change effort. "I want my plant to be known as the plant that produces the highest-quality cars and is most productive! I'm tired of some of the complainers we got round here who don't wanna work. I ain't gonna put up with it no more. Anyone who doesn't get themself to work regularly ain't going to work in my plant!" He meant it. This local union president felt ownership for that plant. It was his. As far as he was concerned, it didn't belong to the thousands of stockholders of Ford Motor Company, the majority of whom wouldn't even know of this plant's existence. It belonged to him, and he took pride in its productivity and quality as he would his own. His feeling of ownership and determination would make the plant successful. And every stockholder of Ford Motor Company should be thankful that Billie Joe Harris feels the sense of ownership they lack, for it is he who will determine the fate of the company.

This psychology of ownership will become an increasingly necessary condition for success. It will become necessary because of the changing nature of work, its management and work force. In the days when work was predominantly mindless toil, it was possible to maintain complete distinctions between those who were owners, those who thought and made decisions, and those who carried out the decisions through their physical labor. The distinction between owner, manager, and worker was a valid one in the industrial age. In the new age this distinction will be a liability and a drag on the success of the firm.

THE SHIFTING VALUE OF LABOR AND CAPITAL

In days past, the capable manager was satisfied to work for the owner, understanding that he worked at the owner's pleasure, enjoying a fair wage but having little stake in the larger success of the firm. Today and in the future, the manager must feel ownership in the organization or he will depart to seek that condition, one which is increasingly available to him. This pattern has been most prevalent in the high-technology firms where technical and managerial competence are the primary ingredients required to start a new company. The dollar capital required to start one of these new firms has been easily available to the manager with the proven technical skills. The ratio of stock ownership maintained by the entrepreneur who brought only his own human capital to the organization is a good indication of the declining value of dollar capital to the total ownership of an organization.

In the industrial age, the capitalist could obtain and control managers. In the information age, the manager is able to obtain and control the capital. The tables are now turning. The capitalist needs the competent manager-leader far more than the manager needs the capitalist. The creation of new firms does not require the volumes of capital required to start new steel, automobile, or other large manufacturing organizations. The financial capital required to create a successful business in the service-information economy is relatively available, yet the human capital, expertise, relatively scarce. Expertise will be unavailable unless the condition of ownership is present. That ownership will have to be of the most genuine kind, the spirit of ownership.

The decentralization of capital is also increasing the ability of the competent individual to command capital. One hundred years ago there were relatively few persons with the ability to organize the large sums of money required to start an enterprise. The capital markets were dominated by a few banks and individual investors. Today the capital markets are dominated by many more institutions, many more individual investors, and many more nations. It is estimated that employees, through their pension funds, are rapidly approaching the ownership of more than 50 percent of the equity capital in the United States. Despite this ownership, which Peter Drucker has dubbed "Equity Fund Socialism," employees exert relatively little influence today over the selection of members of boards of directors and, therefore, over company policy.[1] However, it is likely that employee ownership of corporations through pension funds, as well as via stock distribution through negotiated settlements with corporations, will begin to be felt in the boardroom. At the time of this writing, Eastern Airlines was considering appointing two members of its board based on employee selection. At the same time, employees granted the company another loan through payroll deductions. It is significant that Frank Borman, Chairman of Eastern Airlines, did not go to the stockholders for additional funds, he went to the employees. Membership on the Chrysler Corporation board by a member of the United Auto Workers union is likely to be a permanent position and soon will inevitably be followed by employee representation on the boards of other automobile manufacturers.

The unfortunate aspect of current employee ownership in corporations is that they do not "feel" they are owners nearly to the degree that they possess financial ownership. Most employees, in fact, have little knowledge of the equity held by their pension funds and have virtually no ability to exert any control. Hence they do not experience the connection between their financial investment and their work. While they may own 50 percent of corporate America, they do not feel like 50 percent partners. Because they do not feel this investment, they do not act like owners. The Japanese accomplishment has been in mastering the psychology of ownership. The Japanese employee experiences the spirit of oneness with his firm independent of his financial interest in the company. This feeling of unity is a major explanation for the relatively harmonious labor-management relations in Japan.

OWNERSHIP OR ALIENATION

The worker, increasingly less distinguishable from the manager or the professional, also has increasing options, and the spirit of ownership will be a condition necessary to his motivation. In the preindustrial age, the spirit of ownership was prevalent. The American national economy in its earlier days was dominated by the small farmer and the small craftsman. The small farmer was highly independent and self-reliant. The spirit of ownership was assumed and the product of the simple relationship between the self, work, and rewards. The craftsman and apprentice also felt this close tie to their work, signing and dating their piece of furniture, their immortality preserved in the product of their labor. As small crafts gave way to manufacturing and industrial organizations, the psychological distance between self and work gradually increased. The worker on Henry Ford's assembly line no longer signed his name to his product, no longer determined the rate of production, no longer was given credit for the quality of his work by its recipients. The credit went to the industrialist, designer, and manufacturer. As recognition for the value of the product decreasingly went to the worker, the worker's feelings of self-worth declined. The worker became a nobody, another cog in the productive wheel. As the self was denied appreciation by the work environment, the individual devalued the work. Identity had to be sought elsewhere to preserve individual integrity.

From the alienation produced by the work environment, the union movement was energized. Here was something the worker could control. It was his! It represented him. His ego, rejected by the corporation, found expression in the union. Unfortunately, the union was only a counterforce, not a creative force. It was a force of power and control, but not one serving a creative purpose. The battles between union and corporation were not merely battles over pay and benefits. They were like battles between the will of a parent and the ego of a child who, rejected and trampled upon by the parent, was now turning against the parent, demanding recognition and self-worth. If the organization was not to confer self-esteem through the accomplishment of the work itself, which it did not, the worker would create his own mechanism, his own subculture within which self-esteem would be granted.

The union fulfilled the need for ownership. The worker felt ownership and unity with his union, not with his company. With his company the relationship was adversarial, and this further supported the need for the union. The existence of company and union, management and labor, each balancing the other, enabled a working relationship that met the minimum needs of each.

The relationship we should be seeking is that relationship between capital, management, and labor that results in the most efficient production of wealth, the purpose for which the corporation exists. The maintenance of the adversarial relationship between union and management requires energy diverted from the productive task. The maximization of productivity can be achieved only by acquiring unity of purpose. This will occur when capital, management, and labor are united in the spirit of mutual concern.

JUSTICE AND POWER

Unity of purpose is blocked by our tradition of adversarial problem solving. We tend to believe that in any dispute one party is right and one party is wrong. We have also been taught that in order to prove that you are right in a dispute, you must have and use power. Our culture has taught us that problems are solved by one group or individual opposing and defeating another group or individual. This principle of adversarial problem solving is deep in our roots. It is closely tied to command leadership and is equally a block to consensus decision making.

I recall reading about the Crusades, particularly the Third Crusade, led by Richard the Lion-Hearted. Saladin was the great Muslim leader who captured Jerusalem, bringing about the Crusade. Saladin was honored and respected for his honesty and bravery even by the Christians. In his diary he wrote about a visit he once made to the camp of his adversary, Richard the Lion-Hearted. Saladin, who was used to Muslim courts and system of laws which were far more advanced for their day than were the Christians', was extremely distraught by the scene he witnessed in the Crusaders' camp that night. There had been a dispute between two knights over the ownership of a horse. The dispute was to be settled by trial before the feasting of the occasion. One of the warriors was an old man, obviously weak and frail. The other was a warrior, young and strong. The trial was a simple one. Richard, accompanied by Saladin, sat on a dais overlooking the field on which the trial was to take place. Each knight took up position at opposite ends of the field. Richard gave a command, and the two warriors rushed at each other, swords drawn. Needless to say, it was the younger knight who was left standing when it was over. Clearly he was in the right. The horse belonged to him.

The settling of disputes by force is in our tradition. In order to be protected from exploitation or abuse, we believe that we must have a respected force on our side. The jousting by the knights of the Middle Ages was a means of settling disputes and reestablishing honor if one felt insulted. The word "joust" has the same roots as the word "just." Jousting was a means of establishing justice. As our civilization has progressed, we have become somewhat less prone to the use of physical force to settle disputes, so we no longer joust. However, things have not changed that much. We now perform the joust indoors. We hire specialists to engage in the combat for us, yet the dais is still occupied by the honored berobed person looking down on the field of combat. The lawyers charge at each other, determined to pursue victory with no less vigor than the knights of old. The participant who outwits his opponent is judged to be in the right. Unfortunately, the judgment is still based as much on the play of the game as on the merits of the dispute itself. In many ways the combat to determine justice has progressed little from that which Saladin found so horrifying. Our society is as prone to litigation as the society of feudal Europe was to jousting. Fortunately, the English Church eventually became horrified by the destruction caused by the jousting at tournaments and supported a ban on them by refusing Christian burial to anyone who died in these contests. Some such similar measure may be in order in our own day.

When we feel that we are the subject of injustice, we will organize forces to engage in combat. For this purpose, unions were formed. When the spirit of unity prevails in our corporations, when the one-ness of purpose, interests, and rewards dominate the life of the cor-poration, there will be no need for unions.

THE PATH TO UNITY

The spirit of unity or ownership is being achieved today at an im-pressive rate within our corporations. Sometimes it is brought about by mutual desperation, as in the case of the auto industry and the United Auto Workers, and sometimes because of the actions of an enlightened senior executive.

Preston Trucking practiced the art of adversarial combat as well as any trucking company. The Teamsters' union was equal to the chal-lenge. The company's Detroit terminal, in the heart of Teamster territory, was among the roughest of battle scenes. The Teamsters filed more grievances here than in any other terminal in the com-pany. They worked at an inordinately slow pace, each decision af-fecting workers became a source of prolonged debate and hostility between management and union representatives. The Detroit termi-nal was a money loser. Performance was so poor that the company was considering closing the terminal and retreating from one front of a large battlefield. The Preston management team had enough vision to recognize that those trucking firms that could establish more posi-tive working relations with their employees would be at a competi-tive advantage.

Preston Trucking instituted a training program for all supervisors and terminal managers. The training emphasized the use of positive reinforcement, visualized data-based feedback, listening to em-ployees, and joint problem solving. Each supervisor instituted a project with his team, consisting of his immediate subordinates, whereby he pinpointed one performance that he wished to improve. He set an objective and placed the performance and objective on a graph. He began to give his employees positive feedback, expressing appreciation, sharing the data with them as the performance improved. Within a few months the key performances improved substantially, grievances began to decline, and the operation of the terminal became increasingly profitable. Improved performance had become rewarding for all performers, not just for a group of managers and supervisors.

A number of months after this improvement, Preston executives shared their success story with managers from Caterpillar Tractor. The Caterpillar managers visited the Detroit terminal and met with the rank and file to hear their version of the change that had occurred. The Caterpillar managers listened with some skepticism and finally asked one of the workers, "What was the real reason why you guys did this for Preston Trucking, anyway?" The worker, a hardened and experienced warrior of traditional combat, leaned forward, looked the manager in the eye, and said, "Listen, buddy, we don't work for Preston Trucking. We are Preston Trucking!" The real victory had been achieved. Unity of purpose, ownership, was accomplished.

The psychology of ownership, unity can be achieved, as in the case of the Preston truckers, without any change in contract, compensation, or legal ownership. Ownership is a psychological condition of shared interest between the individual and the organization for which he works. It is the achievement of this unity that must be a priority for today's managers.

What then are the keys to creating this unity? They are first, to design the structure of the organization so as to reduce the unnecessary layers of management and give the greatest possible responsibility to the lowest possible levels of the company. This flattening of the pyramid is now in progress in a number of major corporations such as the Ford Motor Company. Second, compensation systems must be redesigned to create unity of concern rather than accentuate the distinction between management and labor. All employees should be salaried with incentive earnings tied to competence and performance. Third, the greatest degree of involvement and consensus should be sought from all levels. Fourth, and perhaps most important, management must exhibit through their personal style and example the trust and unity that they feel with the employee.

Each of these characteristics can be seen in the example of the Skippy Peanut Butter plant in Little Rock, Arkansas. In this plant of approximately one hundred employees, there are no fixed jobs, no job descriptions, no inspectors or supervisors. There is a general manager, a human resource manager, and a quality assurance manager. The responsibility for meeting production and quality goals rests with all one hundred plant employees. The three managers act as advisers to the employees. The employees are their own supervisors. They have access to all plant data and are regularly briefed on production, costs, demand, and distribution.

When this plant was opened, it was planned as a self-managed environment. When employees were hired, they were given approximately forty hours of "social training" designed to indoctrinate them in the desired culture. Accepting product responsibility was stressed as a tough job which could be undertaken only by people of superior fiber. A team system would replace supervisory control, and it was emphasized that this was no place for prima donnas.

Employees met in groups of five to ten to parcel out work assignments democratically, by vote. Soon individuals were volunteering for specific tasks, eliminating the need for voting. Often, even the unpleasant tasks were volunteered for because the employees knew that these jobs would soon be rotated to others. A competency continuum, twelve step-by-step levels of career development, could be pursued at one's own pace. It was acceptable to remain at any career level, based on one's ability or desire. The philosophy was that "allowing people to grow does not mean you force them to grow." Salary raises were tied to monthly proficiency testing.

The key to the success of this self-management is the functioning of the employee work teams. Each team has its own office space, with reports, charts, and graphs depicting schedules and performance covering the walls. When a team is assigned a task, the members divide it up into manageable units and parcel them out among the employees. Each team elects its own secretary and each appoints coordinators. The coordinators interface with the general manager, human resource manager, and product assurance manager. The product assurance manager provides the teams with quality improvement training and gives them feedback on their quality. One of the favored tasks of the team members is their right to interview and pass judgment on job applicants. The employees are probably tougher interviewers than any personnel department and are particularly concerned with the ability of any new applicant to become a reliable and trustworthy member of their team.

The Skippy experiment has been sufficiently successful that the parent corporation, Best Foods, is now planning to expand the concept to other locations. There are dozens of similar experiments being conducted by our largest corporations. The majority of these experiments have proved the cost benefits of unifying work and management and have resulted in quality and performance superior to those of comparable plants managed in a traditional fashion. During the next few decades, management will be experimenting with alternatives that will attempt to create the spirit of unity and ownership that is an essential element of motivation in the new era.

SIX

The Performance Principle

> The primary law of human behavior is that behavior is a
> function of its consequences. That which is rewarded increases.
> When we learn to reward performance we will have
> performance.

When managers describe the poor performance of subordinates, I often ask them what difference that performance makes to their employees. What does it "matter" to the employee? What rewards will follow exceptional performance? In the view of the employee the answer most often given is that nothing will happen if the employee works harder, faster, or smarter. The manager's life may be somewhat happier as a result of this performance, but the employee's life does not change. This is the most common reason for poor individual performance: There is no perceived reward for improved performance.

The culture and spirit of a corporation are strongly influenced by the tendency of managers not to reinforce good performance or to assume that "that's their job, why should I reward that?" There are tendencies in corporations toward reward or punishment. Those who are best at reinforcing good performance are generally less authoritarian, more participative, and more concerned about the individual. Those who are more prone to the use of punishment tend to be more conditioned by the traditional management culture. Among corporations with which I am familiar, R. J. Reynolds Tobacco, 3M, Honeywell, and IBM all have cultures in which there is a high acceptance of the responsibility to reinforce desirable performance.

I remember when I first visited R. J. Reynolds Tobacco in Winston-Salem, North Carolina. To say that Reynolds is a significant factor in the community of Winston-Salem is as much of an understatement as saying that the federal government is a significant factor

in the community of Washington, D. C. The tobacco plants dominate downtown Winston-Salem and the aroma of tobacco cannot be
missed as you drive by on the expressway.

Will Hanes, vice-president of manufacturing, walked with me
through one of the plants explaining the manufacturing equipment
that spit out cigarettes at a machine-gun pace. The old wooden floors
glistened with a mirrorlike varnish that would be the envy of most
contemporary homemakers. Will Hanes was a large man who had
grown up working for R.J.R. As he walked through the plant, he
called over a woman of about forty and asked how her daddy was
feeling. He knew her father had recently suffered a stroke. She was
an hourly worker and he addressed her by her first name. She returned the courtesy. He walked on and called to a "maintainer."
"Hey, Harold, come over here and tell us about this chart." Harold
walked over, chest out, smiling, obviously proud to explain his
chart. Harold proceeded to give an explanation that, as far as I was
concerned, was entirely too long-winded. But Will listened, nodding
his head, asking questions, apparently genuinely interested. I faked
it. When Harold was done, Will turned to me, with the man listening in, and said, "Harold here is one of the best. This chart was his
idea." Turning back to Harold, Will said, "You keep that up,
Harold," and we left him just a little more proud than before.

Back in Will Hanes's office I sat talking with him, but was dis-
tracted by the collection of books on the credenza behind his desk.
The collection included a variety of volumes, among them Dr.
Seuss's *Sneetches and Other Stories.* I knew *Sneetches* because I had two
young children to whom I frequently read this and other Dr. Seuss
favorites. *Sneetches* is the story of Star-Bellied Sneetches who walked
upon beaches, obviously quite superior to other Sneetches without
stars upon thars. It is certainly one of the most clever and simple
lessons in prejudice. This book also contains the story of the North-
Going Zaks and the South-Going Zaks who meet head-on and get
stuck in their tracks because they learned, in Zaks school, that a
Zaks never deviates from his tracks. I finally broke out in laughter
and had to ask for an explanation. Will explained that when he had
problems with employees who refused to solve problems in a cooperative manner, who failed to appreciate the other person's point of
view, he would bring them into his office and have them read the
appropriate story. Surely one of the most unique but undoubtedly
effective correcting procedures I have encountered.

R. J. Reynolds Tobacco was characterized by genuine human concern. It is not so much a corporation as it is a community, a church, a family. Everyone knows everyone else and, at least as observed by an outsider, genuinely appears to care. For this reason it took little training and assistance on our part to cause managers to "catch someone doing something good." Positive reinforcement was a natural and easy refinement of their already positive environment. Productivity in these plants was excellent, and it improved still more as rewards and recognition were applied just a bit more skillfully.

One of the overwhelming facts of organizational life is that we are all chasing rewards. No, the carrot and stick are not dead. Appearing in a never-ending variety of sizes, shapes, and colors, yes. But dead they are not.

A FUNCTION OF CONSEQUENCES

Every institution controls rewards and punishments and cannot escape the responsibility of administering those consequences. Promotions, salaries, bonuses, stock options, perks, job security, status, recognition, praise, educational opportunity are all forms of reward that are distributed daily by every corporation. These are the costs of doing business. There is a returned benefit and that benefit is individual performance. The cost-benefit relationship is a function of the contingent relationship ("If A is performed, then B will be given as a consequence") between performance and reinforcement. The unfortunate fact is that our institutions are terribly poor at this administration, and they are most incompetent at the bottom of the ladder and at the top.

Following college, the first institution I worked in was the prison for young adults in Raleigh, North Carolina, mentioned earlier. I was the sole counselor for three hundred and fifty young inmates. I attempted one-on-one counseling with some of my charges. However, it didn't take me very long to realize that my ability to influence their behavior during a one-hour-per-week counseling session was of minuscule import compared with the power of the environment in which they spent the remainder of the week. Their behavior was well controlled by a disciplined system of reward and punishment. Unfortunately, the staff had little to do with the control of that system. It was a system entirely controlled by the inmates. Inmates had their own hierarchy of power, status, privilege, and even material and sexual rewards. The staff controlled little of any genuine importance to the inmates.

I soon gave up on individual counseling in exchange for an attempt at managing the total environment. With the help of a federal grant and with an understanding of the elementary principles of behavior modification, I redesigned another prison of one hundred and fifty serious young offenders.

In this institution there were four dormitories that were all the same. I redesigned them as luxury, quality, standard, and efficiency dorms, differentiated by amenities such as televisions, carpets, curtains, and late-hour privileges. However, not believing in the proverbial free lunch, we started charging rent. No more free board in this prison. We paid every inmate with a personal check for the work they did each week in the prison industry, and we charged them for everything worthwhile in the living area. We set up a bank and all transactions were by check. We even charged for overdrafts. All payments were in "points," no real dollars were involved. However, these points had every value that a dollar has in the free society. All of a sudden we had a real economy, with inmates being evaluated on the job each week and paid according to their supervisors' judgment of their performance; they were writing out checks for movies, rent, use of the canteen, and any other privilege. Before this system went into effect, the amount or quality of work done by an inmate genuinely did not matter. There were no desirable consequences for performance. Suddenly the consequences were quite like those of the real world. With the system, inmates could learn to earn, compete, save, impress their boss, and make spending choices and suffer the consequence of poor choices, all skills they had not learned before coming to prison.

I found it interesting that the inmates loved this system. They enjoyed earning. The institution now controlled some consequences to behavior that mattered to them and they were therefore able to manage their behavior in a more positive manner. Punishment became less frequent because of the positive motivation to earn. Production in the industrial area nearly doubled; accidents, machine breakdowns, idleness all declined dramatically. Even these inmates, all of whom were there for serious crimes, would respond with high performance, motivation, and dedicated work to a system that recognized their good performance, a system that made it matter.

Shortly after this experience I began working in the industrial set-ting and found, to my surprise, that the effectiveness of rewards and recognition in the corporate setting was, although better than in most prisons, not terribly effective. Most employees are paid to be present, and contrary to Woody Allen's line that "eighty percent of success is showing up," only 20 percent of productivity is showing up. Desiring to perform at an exceptional level is 80 percent of pro-ductivity. Eighty percent of the desire to perform is a function of the consequences, the rewards and punishments, that make performance matter.

THE POWER PRINCIPLE

The majority of employees in this country are not paid for any mea-sure of performance. The majority are paid for seniority, for the status of a craft or profession, or for the degree to which they are organized to wield power. Power is the dominant principle by which rewards are currently dispensed. Power may be derived from the scarcity of a skill, from the effectiveness by which the workers are organized, or from the workers' ability to cause damage by strikes or laxity on the job. That power pays is a corollary of the adversarial axiom of the corporations. Those who manage the organization have made this assumption correct. You will not experience a significant advance in what you earn without wielding power against the com-pany. We are teaching this lesson still.

No organization in America should be of greater concern than our elementary and secondary schools. Yet in no other set of institutions is the power principle more clearly evident. In most communities teachers are paid less than garbage collectors, police, and firemen, less than clerks and secretaries. Yet it is the teachers to whom we entrust the care and education of our most prized possessions, our children, our future. Only in those communities or regions of the country where teachers are organized in unions are they able to com-mand respectable salaries. In most of the country it is literally im-possible to raise a family on the salary of a teacher. So who will remain a teacher? Will it be the brightest and best? Of course not. Only those with enormous dedication and some additional source of income, or those with a poor self-image and a standard of mediocrity will remain in that neglected profession. Teachers lack power. It is to our own detriment that they did not recognize their impotence earlier and put up a more respectable fight. Their ranks in many parts of the United States (the South, where I live, qualifies) are made up of those willing to accept secondary roles and life-styles, and who lack the strength of character necessary to organize and fight the fight that must be fought if there is to be a resurgence in education in this country.

Because the population of teachers is largely composed of individuals with low personal standards, they have developed enormous resistance to any form of compensation that differentiates based on performance. This despite the fact that should be obvious to any teacher who has studied the principles of learning, that performance is a function of its consequences whether among schoolchildren, teachers, inmates, workers, or executives.

Our corporations and other organizations dispense justice. Justice is not only the province of the courts. Justice is built upon the twin pillars of rewards and punishment. Justice occurs when either rewards or punishment are administered in a manner that is related to actual performance and in a measure that is culturally acceptable. We consider that justice has been done when a court sentences someone who actually did the crime and when the punishment is considered to be of comparable severity to the crime. If the wrong person is sentenced, or if the sentence is too harsh or too lenient, we consider the outcome to be unjust. The same criteria apply to rewards. When the right employee is promoted, that employee who has performed best or who can reasonably be expected to perform best in the new position, we consider this to be fair. We also consider a raise, bonus, or award to be equitable if it is in some reasonable proportion to performance. Again, if either criteria, the right person or a reasonable measure, are violated, we consider the outcome to be unjust.

It is our corporations which dispense more in the way of rewards than any other institution in our society. Their ability to administer those rewards to the right people, and in a measure that is appropriate, determines their own claim to be just and, in large measure, accounts for the perception that society is either just or unjust. It is therefore essential that corporations strive to administer rewards and punishments in the most just manner possible. As we expect justice to control acceptable behavior in society, so too will justice control desirable behavior in corporations. It is just that as employees perform faster, smarter, or more creatively, they are rewarded. It is not just that employees be compensated at increasingly higher rates due to seniority or other contractual stipulations when their performance is declining.

PAY FOR PERFORMANCE

Pay for performance practices are not new. Lincoln Electric Company in Euclid, Ohio, has been paying for performance since 1934. Lincoln has become well known for its announcements of annual bonuses to employees. It is common for the annual bonus to equal the annual salary of the employee. In 1982 bonuses dipped considerably as a result of the economic downturn that affected Lincoln, whose products are primarily industrial electrical motors. The annual bonuses dipped to an average of $15,000 per worker from an average of $22,690 a year earlier! The company paid out $41.2 million to 2,634 employees, a decline of $18 million.

Lincoln's bonus system is based on a number of factors. "Seniority means nothing here," said George E. Willis, the president. The bonus is based on piecework, attention to quality, and a merit rating system that reviews every worker every six months. The bonus system is impacted also by the profits of the company. Lincoln has evolved a system to pay for those performances which it regards as most critical. Through its tracking system, the firm can trace errors in quality to the individual employee. A mistake on a product that actually gets to a customer can result in a $1,500 penalty for a worker, even though the item may only sell for $100. Lincoln's quality and productivity are so high that no foreign firm has made any significant inroads into its market. This emphasis on performance has enabled the firm to practice a policy of job security. No one has been laid off from Lincoln Electric since 1949. Last year when business was in a slump, fifty-one employees from the factory and offices were retrained to take on selling jobs. Donald F. Hastings, vice-president for sales, reported that the firm would reap more than $10 million in new sales during the year from this effort. Lincoln has clearly created a culture in which employees feel that they are rewarded for performance, yet the firm has also demonstrated its willingness to sacrifice for its employees when times are bad, and employees return this consideration with high performance and flexibility.

Plans to share in productivity gains and performance are becoming increasingly popular in the United States, and this trend should continue as one component of the larger effort to produce cultures of excellence in our corporations. The implementation of these plans is consistently accompanied by increases in productivity.

There are three plans that are most widely used: the Scanlon Plan, the Rucker Plan, and Improshare. They are all founded on the same philosophy, the philosophy of "gain sharing." Gain sharing is based on the precept of a cooperative culture in which management and labor have an equal or comparable stake in the well-being of the firm, and on the principle that it is fair to share in the gains from harder, smarter, or more creative work. The advocates of each of these plans and those who have experienced their implementation all report that the plan alone will not create the desired result unless the fundamental relationship and communication between management and labor are characterized by trust and respect.

The Scanlon Plan was developed in 1936 by Joe Scanlon of the United Steelworkers at the Empire Steel and Tinplate Company in Mansfield, Ohio. Scanlon was the local president of the Steelworkers union and persuaded the president of Empire Steel to implement a system of employee involvement in order to save the failing company. Initially the program was very successful and enabled Empire to match the rest of the industry. However, the plan that Scanlon later helped to implement at the Adamson Company in East Palatine, Ohio, represents the prototype of the current-day Scanlon Plan.

The Scanlon Plan measures productivity improvement by a change in the computed ratio of total payroll dollars divided by the total dollar sales value of production. Most Scanlon Plans distribute 75 percent of the gains to employees and 25 percent to the company. Usually, 25 percent of the monthly gains are placed into a pool to absorb the loss for poor months. At the end of the year the entire pool is distributed. Scanlon Plans also include a highly structured suggestion program with joint employee-management committees that review suggestions and decide on awards. There are many modifications of the Scanlon Plan, most incorporating other ratios to determine payouts to the employee.

The Rucker Plan was developed in the late 1940s by Allan W. Rucker of the Eddy-Rucker-Nickels Company in Cambridge, Massachusetts. The major difference between the Scanlon and Rucker plans is in the measurement formula. The Rucker Plan relies on a measure of productivity as the ratio between dollar payroll and dollar value added. The output figure used is sales less materials purchased. Both the Rucker and Scanlon plans are based on single measures of gain, and therefore can present problems unless there is a well-understood agreement as to when and how the ratios will be adjusted for unanticipated factors such as technology changes.

Improshare was developed in 1974 by Mitchell Fein, an industrial engineer with experience in traditional incentive systems. It was designed to eliminate the problems associated with individual incentive plans normally instituted by industrial engineers. It is based on the establishment of a goal to produce more units of a finished product in fewer man-hours worked. Each employee is treated as a member of a work group or team, and productivity is indexed by the group's output of finished product, not by the individual's output. This obviously helps foster teamwork and peer pressure to perform. The gains from improved productivity are shared by company and labor fifty-fifty.

In 1981 the General Accounting Office completed a study of gain-sharing programs to determine if they contributed to productivity improvement. The report estimated that approximately one thousand gain-sharing plans are now in effect in this country. The GAO reported that "among the 24 firms providing financial data, those with a productivity plan in effect the longest showed the best performance. Firms that had plans in operation over 5 years averaged almost 29% savings in work force costs for the most recent 5 year period. Those firms with plans in operation less than 5 years averaged savings of 8.5%." Also cited were nonfinancial gains. Improved labor relations were reported by 80.6 percent of those responding; fewer grievances by 47.2 percent; less absenteeism by 36.1 percent and the same percentage reported less turnover. Most of those participating in the GAO study reported that they had experienced the anticipated gains and believed that they had obtained a competitive advantage through the implementation of their gain-sharing plans.

THE REWARDS OF THE GAME

While monetary rewards for performance are an obvious need and contribute to a productive environment, they do not represent the answer. Financial rewards should be part of a total emphasis on performance. This emphasis starts with measurement. There must be measures of performance within the organization that let each person know how he or she is doing, not rated against an arbitrary and artificial standard, but against the only standard that matters: the individual's or group's prior performance. In athletics the emphasis on numbers, batting averages, earned-run averages, number of consecutive games in which a player had a hit, etc., constitutes the primary motive force that captures the interest not only of players but of spectators as well. If you were to observe baseball or any other sport without any reference whatsoever to numbers, it would immediately become one of the more boring and senseless exhibitions imaginable.

There is a myth that people don't like to be measured. On the contrary, people love to be measured. No one objects to measurement in athletics. Who would play golf, who would bowl if there were no scorekeeping? Workers do not like to be measured when they perceive that they are more likely to be punished for nonperformance than rewarded for improved performance. The problem with measurement is in the consequence that follows measurement. Measurement itself results in pure feedback. Pure feedback is in itself positively reinforcing. This is why everyone I have met who has been able to maintain a routine of running or jogging has developed a personal scorekeeping system. They keep track of the number of miles run per week, average minutes per mile, pulse rate at the end of a number of miles, and so forth. Running is certainly one of the most simple activities imaginable. There is no need to keep score. Yet all dedicated runners do keep score. They do it so that they know when they have beaten their past record, an obviously rewarding experience. They keep score so they can validate their feeling that they are doing better or worse. They keep score so that they can have some measure against which it is possible to set an objective. All these activities are naturally reinforcing.

Each manager should ask him- or herself, "When was the last time one of my employees set a personal record?" Why do we not know this? We may have an employee who has just set the all-time corporate record for number of widgets produced in a day, number produced without defect, number of days in attendance in a row, etc. These excellent performances are occurring in our organizations and we are ignoring them. No one is applauding the champion who has dedicated himself to excellence! Why then should anyone be dedicated to such excellence?

A small bit of attention to improved performance can often produce an unbelievable betterment. About eight years ago my associates were working in the textile mills of South Carolina. We asked each manager and supervisor to identify one specific performance that they would like to improve. We then provided a model for analyzing the behavior that comprised this performance and for pinpointing the feedback and reinforcement that could be used to improve the specified performance. This action plan was implemented by each supervisor.

One of the earliest examples of such an action plan was dramatic. Mary was an hourly employee in a textile mill. She worked on a job that had engineered standards. She had been performing at the remarkably low level of 35 percent of standard operating efficiency. Her performance was tolerated because she was very reliable, had a perfect attendance record, and the plant had a very bad attendance problem overall. However, plant attendance had begun to improve and Mary's long-standing low performance had become increasingly unacceptable. The supervisor graphed her performance and showed Mary the graph. He asked her whether she thought she could make some improvement. She said she thought she could. He asked her to set a goal. She set a goal of 45 percent. Each day the supervisor showed her the dot on the graph that represented her performance. Within one week Mary had hit 45 percent. Then the supervisor repeated the procedure.

This attention to Mary and her performance, with no negative comments or criticism, simply showing her how she was doing graphically, asking her to set a goal, and praising her improvement, continued until Mary had achieved the level of 120 percent of standard operating efficiency! She maintained this level for several months. Everyone, including Mary, was amazed. Mary was more than amazed. She was proud.

This is the type of reward that is most valuable and lacking. Attention to measured performance in a positive manner, focusing on individual record setting have enormous impact on performance. There is no reward more powerful than genuine appreciation.

RESPONSIBILITY AT THE TOP

Performance contingent rewards are not only needed at the bottom of the corporation, they are needed at the top. If the corporation is to be viewed as "just," the senior managers must include themselves in the performance criteria for compensation. In July 1982, *Fortune* magazine published a study of the compensation of chief executive officers of U.S. corporations to determine whether remuneration at the top was related to performance. They reported that "in a totally rational world, top executives would get paid handsomely for first-class performance, and would lose out when they flopped. But to an extraordinary extent, those who flop still get paid handsomely. In this regard, they have something in common with union members who are able to extract higher-than-market wages from their employers."

Fortune published charts that depicted the relationship of pay to performance. These charts, by industry, plotted the performance of the corporation on one axis (as measured by return on stockholders' equity) and total CEO compensation on the other axis. Simply stated, there is no apparent correlation between these two measurements among executives of most industries. Walton R. Winder, a Towers, Perrin, Forster & Crosby compensation consultant, reported that his firm's studies show that a correlation between size of corporation and pay is relatively high, and the correlation between pay and performance is weak. Another consultant, Louis J. Brindisi, Jr., of Booz, Allen & Hamilton, says his studies indicate that performance does not correlate to pay at all. *Fortune* magazine reached the conclusion that "if directors behaved responsibly, they would handle the stockholders' money as if it were their own, avoiding compensation excesses. So many examples of near-unarguable excess exist that a lot of directors must be thought guilty of falling down on the job, perhaps in part because they are often themselves corporate executives and therefore beneficiaries of the system."

What *Fortune* refers to as the "madness of the system" when describing chief executives' pay cannot be rationally defended if one starts with the basic assumption that pay and performance should be related. I doubt that any of the chief executives in the *Fortune* study would question the validity of this most elementary of all principles of good management. However, as is the case among other groups in society, it is most difficult to treat oneself with justice. That is exactly what chief executives must do first if they are to succeed in creating systems at lower levels that reward managers and employees based on performance.

The importance of financial compensation tied to performance is, again, not the entire answer to creating a culture in which performance is prized. Senior, sophisticated managers are equally responsive to the intangible recognition and sincere acknowledgment of their work as any other employee in the organization. Several years ago Honeywell's Aerospace and Defense Group was competing for a Defense Department contract for the next generation of the U.S. torpedo. Honeywell had initially been selected as one of five firms to do development design and engineering work on the torpedo. A team of several hundred engineers and scientists were put to work on the project, which could be worth many millions of dollars over the next decade. Following a year of development work, the designs were judged and two were selected for parallel competitive development. Honeywell's was one of the two.

The Honeywell team worked for another year on the development of prototype models and detailed engineering. Every member of the team was well aware that success of this program meant hundreds of jobs for their corporation for the next decade. They worked an intense schedule of nights and weekends in a true team spirit of competition. The day of judgment came, and the senior executives of Honeywell, including Warde Wheaton, the Aerospace and Defense Group executive, were in Washington to receive the judgment of the Defense Department. They won.

The executives left the meeting, filled with the thrill of victory, and walked down the street, past an ice cream stand. Warde Wheaton stopped and bought everyone an ice cream cone. He told his fellow executives jokingly that the ice cream was a reward for their victory. As the group of executives continued to walk along joking, licking their cones, reflecting on their victory, the marketing executive, Ron Barnhart, decided to rent an ice cream truck, and he had the truck driven to Honeywell's Washington offices, where he bought all of those who were involved in the project an ice cream cone. Photographs were taken of the team responsible for the effort, all holding their cones up in the air.

Today that team is scattered throughout Honeywell, assigned to dozens of different projects. However, as you walk through offices at Honeywell you will spot the same picture on the walls of those managers. The picture is of a large group of grown men, all smiling, all holding ice cream cones high in the air. No explanation of this event is adequate to convey the spirit, teamwork, sense of achievement, and true appreciation conveyed by that photograph of the team and those ice cream cones.

SEVEN

The Empiricism Principle

> The primary task of the manager is to think. The future success of the corporation is dependent upon his ability to think clearly, critically, and creatively.

In times past it is true that the manager or leader was responsible for demonstrating the behavior that was desired, setting an example of the productive skill. Military leaders fought. The head carpenter demonstrated woodworking skills to his men. Rarely now does a manager demonstrate the productive skill of the enterprise, other than that of thinking, the most critical of all productive skills. The business of the future will succeed on the ability of its members to think industriously.

Thomas J. Watson, the brilliant past president of IBM, understood that his company would succeed, not on the deployment of assets, not on a brilliance of marketing or engineering, but on his employees' singular ability to use their minds well. He had the word "THINK" hung prominently in every plant and office as if it were a religious icon, as a constant reminder of what was really important. Whenever he spoke at a meeting, the word hung somewhere behind him as if to tell the audience, "If you don't hear anything I say, at least remember to THINK." Watson was creating a cultural tradition, a cultural value, a definition of desired behavior upon which he knew his company must be built. He succeeded. Thinking well is the activity that has made IBM great, and it continues to be its dominant cultural characteristic.

American society is doing a perfectly terrible job of encouraging us to develop our mental faculties. We are all to blame for this. We are supposed to learn to think in school. Our school systems are suffering from neglect and disinterest. We are getting what we have been willing to pay for! Very little. Most of the people teaching our children are good-hearted souls but not among the most skilled at the use of the cerebral cortex. Our education system is a total disgrace, and business and industry, as well as every other institution which requires persons with well-developed mental faculties, are suffering. If our corporations wished to attack the most fundamental cause of productivity problems, they would rush down to the local elementary and primary schools and offer direct assistance. I intend that as a serious proposal.

If anyone questions the severity of the problem, consider the following: The New York Stock Exchange in a study of Japanese and United States productivity concluded that the first cause of the high rate of productivity of Japanese business and the weakness of U.S. business was the differences in the primary and secondary school systems of the two countries.[1] Among the research findings they cited the following:

• Approximately 95 percent of Japanese students graduate from high school. Approximately 74 percent of U.S. students do so.
• Japanese schools are in session five and a half days a week and for more weeks a year. By the time Japanese students have graduated from high school, they have the equivalent of four more years of schooling than do U.S. students.
• An international study of achievement in mathematics reported scores of students in twelve countries on standardized math tests. Japan scored highest with 31.2 and a coefficient of variation of .542. United States students were second from the bottom with a score of 16.2 and a variation coefficient of .821. Japanese students scored almost twice as high in math as U.S. students. The variation coefficients say something about the consistency and predictability of the two educational systems. There is far less variation in Japan.
• In a survey conducted by Tokyo's Nikko Research Center among Japanese companies with U.S. operations, 65 percent of the respondents said that productivity in their American plants was lower than in their Japanese plants. And without exception they blamed that fact in large part on the inferior education and job skills of American workers.[2]

There are many other such facts, but why go on? Virtually no one will argue that U.S. education is superior. Most of us who have recently had children in the public school system can testify to its incompetence. Until recently, however, business, economists, and others who have a great deal to say about how financial resources are allocated have not viewed the problem as having much effect on the bottom line. We had best begin realizing that how well we educate our children is very much an issue of economics, business, and military preparedness.

THE MATH LESSON

It is in the teaching of mathematics where the greatest problem is to be found. What is mathematics? Is it merely addition, subtraction, multiplication, and division of numbers? My recollection of high school math is just that. I don't believe it was ever made clear to me that mathematics is practical problem solving. Mathematics is a process of thinking about things in an orderly fashion. Mathematics is decision making. One cannot possibly be an effective decision maker in the workplace if one is ignorant and incompetent at mathematics.

When I was in high school I had a friend named Allen. Allen was often failing math or barely getting by. He hated math (so did I) and found it incomprehensible. Allen was far more devoted to baseball. It was the Brooklyn Dodgers in those days, and Allen knew the score every day they played. He also knew the batting average of every player. He knew their lifetime averages, their career highest averages, their lowest; the number of home runs hit by each this year, last year, and lifetime, etc. He could also tell you how the Dodgers had played against each opponent, whether they were on an upward or a downward trend, and therefore what the probability was of their winning any given game. Allen loved to bet. All but the most foolish, however, learned that if you bet against Allen you were betting against the odds, because he knew them. Allen was poor at math in the classroom because it had little to do with anything of interest. It represented meaningless toil. However, when it came to something that mattered, he had no problem at all using numbers. I have no doubt that today Allen may be a successful manager, if not a bookie.

It is the ability to use fundamental mathematical concepts in business decision making and to use a general "attitude of science," empiricism, that is a critical issue in the profitability of businesses. An attitude of science is pragmatic questioning. It is the intellectual curiosity to ask why something is supposedly "known." To ask for the data that justify an assumption. It is the opposite of mental laziness. It is the ability to recognize that when the commercial on television proclaims that "more doctors recommend the ingredients in Anacin," it is actually stating that more doctors recommend aspirin and do not recommend Anacin (aspirin being the primary ingredient in Anacin, of course). But most of us have become so accustomed to sloppy thinking and have so few demands placed on us to use our intellects for other than video absorption, that we are in serious danger of becoming a nation of intellectual inferiors. Teaching Americans to think empirically is, I believe, a key dimension of the necessary new culture of American corporations if those corporations are to compete in the world arena.

Managers do not think well. I am constantly amazed at the absence of fundamental logic and the failure to use the most basic mathematical tools. I recently spent a day at a plant that produced a consumer food product. The plant manager and his team were asked to identify a set of "things they would like to see different" in the plant if they had the power to cause everyone to behave exactly as they would like them to. The flip chart in front of them was divided down the middle with "nonmeasurable" written on one side of the page and "measurable" written on the other. They had listed eight nonmeasurable things they would like to see changed in the plant before one said, "I guess we should have some measurable objectives, too?" Then they identified absenteeism as an objective. They all agreed that this was a serious problem. I asked them what attendance or absenteeism was running at in the plant. Nobody knew. They had no idea whether it ran at 5 percent, 10 percent, 15 percent, or 20 percent. They thought there were records from which the data could be figured out, but none of them had bothered to do this. Yet this turned out to be the only measurable performance they wished to change!

It is most typical for managers to know a measure of their key performance responsibilities, the recent performance, some target performance, and likely some benchmark criteria from the past. However, they usually do not know whether the data are trending upward or down; they do not know the mean performance over any recent interval of time; and they have no idea as to what the variability in performance or standard deviation is from the mean.

Knowledge of statistically measurable performance may be the most fundamental of all management skills. Almost all American managers are deficient in this skill. There is a myth that American managers are too numbers oriented. This is nonsense. American managers may have too many disorganized and confusing numbers in their possession, and they may use those numbers to justify decisions. Their decisions may be poor, but it is not because they have used numbers and failed to use their intuition. They have failed to understand the numbers they have in their possession, they do not know how to use them for decision making, and for this reason their intuition is not well developed. When you are uncertain of a decision, it is quite easy to find a number that appears to justify the decision.

THE MOTIVATION OF MEASUREMENT

At all levels, employees will perform measurably better when they know how they are performing. An apparel plant in North Carolina had trained its managers in the use of feedback and positive reinforcement. The supervisors discussed their work teams' performance with the employees each week in a team meeting. Each supervisor showed the employees the graph paper on which he was plotting the team's performance each day. The employees asked for permission to make a similar graph on the wall of the work area. They received permission and proceeded to make a graph that was about four feet high. When I saw the graph it extended about thirty feet to the right. The workers had plotted their production each day for about one full year. More interesting were the comments and artwork that appeared at each significant peak and valley. At peaks there were comments such as "First time to hit 8,700 ever!" "New record for 1982," etc. There were smiling faces and sad faces at peaks and valleys. As I stood looking at the graph, a couple of hourly workers were walking by and I stopped them to ask for their explanation of some of the recent highs and some of the past lows. They were very aware of what had happened on different dates. Referring to a dip on the graph, one of the employees commented that "we ain't gonna let that happen again, we took care of that problem." And then another worker pointed to the goal which they hoped to reach by the end of the month, a red line extending forward on the graph. What was obvious in talking with these employees was that this graph was their scoreboard. They gained pleasure from watching the line progress upward, and experienced pain when it dipped. Perhaps more important, they were doing what management is usually incompetent to do: They were involved in the analysis of cause. The graph was the tool that enabled and motivated them to analyze cause. This is the effect of graphing and charting, one of the most neglected yet powerful and inexpensive management tools available.

A recent cartoon in *The Wall Street Journal* showed two cavemen standing in front of a cave, their clubs over their shoulders. Behind them on the wall at the entrance to the cave is a graph with the line progressing upward. One caveman says to the other, "I don't understand it, but every time I look at it, it just makes me feel good."

DR. W. EDWARDS DEMING

Every manager must know and understand Dr. W. Edwards Deming's contribution to management. Deming, a statistician, was a member of General Douglas McArthur's team assigned to assist in the reconstruction of Japan. Deming did his job. Today in Japan the highest award for quality is the Deming prize. He is often credited as the "father of Japanese quality and productivity." Anyone given this much credit by the Japanese deserves to be listened to with open ears. A number of the largest American corporations have begun to listen.

Dr. Deming has been consulting with the Ford Motor Company on the application of his statistical process control techniques and philosophy. Deming will not work with a corporation unless the most senior management becomes personally involved. Donald Peterson, Ford's president, obliged. I recently viewed a videotape message recorded by Peterson for viewing by all Ford management personnel. The essential message of the tape was the following: "I have been studying and applying Dr. Deming's principles and techniques and I believe that they are the key to our achieving our goals for quality and productivity. I expect the rest of you to do the same." This tape left little doubt that the Ford manager concerned about his career would learn to demonstrate competence in Deming's techniques. Since that time, Ford has sent a letter to each of its approximately 6,000 suppliers informing them that it intends to reduce the total number of suppliers to approximately 3,000 (Deming taught Ford that the more suppliers, the more difficulty there is in achieving statistical control of input quality), and that a major criterion for the selection of suppliers would be their use of statistical methods to manage quality. This message is very good news because it will do much to heighten the awareness of statistical methods.

What is it that Dr. Deming teaches? His teachings are not merely a few simple quality-control techniques, although they are built on this foundation. He teached a philosophy of management. His philosophy demands that managers assume responsibility for performance, rather than pass blame on to subordinates, and learn to analyze the causes of performance and nonperformance. Deming insists that managers think empirically about performance, and he gives them a method for going about it.[3]

Dr. Deming insists that the first task is to achieve statistical control for any process. This must be accomplished before the system can be improved, and it is a significant step toward improved quality. For example, if the data are trending up or down, there is no point attempting to change the system because one does not know the system's real performance. The system is not stable, and until it has achieved stability, no one can say what performance will be produced by it. It is much like judging the value of a piece of equipment before it is properly set up and running according to its own specifications. The machine's performance is fluctuating based on a trial-and-error effort to establish its proper setup. Only when it is properly set up and producing stable performance is it under control and only then can improvements in the system be made.

To determine whether a process is within statistical control, the data on the performance must be plotted, control limits established, and variations reduced by the elimination of "special causes." Dr. Deming says that until this stability and elimination of variation are achieved, there will be no system. "Stability, or the existence of a system, is seldom a natural state. It is an achievement, the result of eliminating special causes one by one on statistical signal, leaving only the random variations of a stable process."[4] Once a stable state is achieved, then the performance of the system is known (before that, it is unknown), and only then should efforts be made to improve the system. Efforts to improve the system before it is within control actually increase the variation in performance, assuring that the system will stay out of control and assuring poor quality.

Most American managers, of course, have no idea as to whether the systems they manage are within control or not. They also do not know whether their actions serve to increase or decrease their systems' stability. A division general manager responsible for fourteen manufacturing plants has the habit of reviewing the production data from each plant every day. He has a general idea of what the previous data have been from each plant, and he has a goal for the production level for each. If the day's numbers represent progress toward the goal, or if they are approximately what they have been in the recent past, he will do nothing. If, however, the numbers show less than this, he will telephone the plant manager and demand to know what went wrong and what the manager plans to do about it. Of course, he has no idea whether the number that concerns him represents a statistic within the limits of system control or whether it represents a "special cause." When the plant manager receives the call, he knows that he must do something to pacify his division manager. He must make some change and he does. In fact, the performance that concerns the division manager may represent random variations produced by the system (this is often the case in this example). The plant manager's action to change something at this point will only throw the system out of control, increasing variation and reducing overall performance.

If the manager knew that the system was in control, he would not respond to one point of data. He would respond to the total system performance. Managers often overlook the very elementary fact that approximately one half of all points of data fall below the mean of those points. At any time one half of every machine in a plant is running at below-average performance. This will be true no matter how good the performance of the machines, workers, or plant. What is significant is whether the performance is within statistical control. If the below-average performance is within control limits, it represents a random variation within the system.

Our division manager should help the plant manager analyze how the system might be changed to improve performance overall. Understanding system performance and system cause leads to rational problem solving, rather than to blaming. Dr. Deming: "Why do you need figures? Not to know if there is a problem. People already know if there's a problem. Not to know the extent of the problem. Knowing the magnitude of the problem doesn't help you to solve the problem. Instead you need figures to know if you need to change the system."

Sloppy thinking is not merely a problem for management. Our culture promotes sloppy thinking. Consider the following from *The Wall Street Journal* (September 14, 1981): "NRC STUDY RATES 15 NUCLEAR PLANTS 'BELOW AVERAGE': Washington—Nuclear reactors at 15 of the nation's 50 power plant sites have failed on a Nuclear Regulatory Commission 'report card' and will get closer attention from federal inspectors. The NRC staff, based on studies concluded at the end of last year, found the 15 power plants 'below average' in overall performance, including maintenance, radiation and fire protection and management control."[5] Obviously fifteen power plants were below average. In fact, the number below average must have been much closer to twenty-five, given that approximately one half of any set of numbers fall below the mean of those numbers. By this criterion about one half of any group will always be victims of the average and open to rebuke and, in this case, probably public protest demonstrations.

Deming distinguishes between common causes and special causes. Common causes are those within the system and, he claims, are responsible for 85 percent of the variation in performance. The system is the responsibility of management. Blaming workers for the variations within system performance is useless because they do not control the design of the system. Managers change systems, and managers must act to analyze and improve those systems. Special causes are those sources of variability which are attributable to a certain worker, machine, or particular condition. The discovery and removal of special causes should be the responsibility of on-line supervision and production workers. Special causes are indicated on a control chart when the data are beyond the established control limits.

Dr. Deming insists that it is this attention to performance and, in particular, to quality through statistical measures that is the cause of superior quality in Japanese industry. Until we learn to apply these statistical means at every level of the corporation, we will not be able to match the Japanese.

CRUNCHING NUMBERS FOR ACTION

Thomas J. Peters and Robert H. Waterman have pointed out that excellent managers have a "bias for action."[6] I suspect that it might be stated more accurately that excellent managers have a "bias for rational action." Dr. Deming gives managers a method for analyzing data and determining when action is called for and what type of action is called for. But Deming insists that this method has worked in Japan because the most senior executives have accepted their responsibility for managing and have utilized the techniques and made sure that they were used throughout their firms. Executives think because they have computers crunching numbers by the millions that they are managing their data. Most have little concept of their data. Deming sums it up: "The great men plot data points. Lesser men use computers."

It is computers that should have helped managers understand and utilize data. However, something has gone seriously wrong in the use of computers. Data-processing departments seem to have the objective of causing the largest possible amount of data to flow into the fewest possible hands. They fail to understand a few simple facts about human behavior and management. In the future, computers will be used more productively to help improve performance by the application of the following principles:

1. Data are most valuable at their point of origin. The person or team of workers who generate a number through their work are the ones who can make best use of that number. The objective of the computer should be to help them use that number in the best possible way. Generally, the computer gobbles up the number and the worker never sees it again.

2. Data are most helpful when represented graphically. People who design computer programs and systems are trained to deal with numbers and computers, not to manage other people. They do not understand that most individuals look at a string of numbers and see nothing. The same people look at a graph and can instantly explain the trend, the distance to a goal line, the number of times the goal has been met, the variability of the data. This leads to action, and it is precisely for the creation and management of such action that data systems and computers exist.

3. The value of data is directly related to their timeliness. In the

future the delay between the generation of a point of data and its representation on a terminal will be eliminated. Workers will have immediate access to terminals which will display all their relevant data.

4. The computer will generate a simple report of the five to ten numbers that each manager should be concerned with. No manager should have to deal with a hundred or a thousand numbers. These figures may be available as backup and for research; however, he must have presented to him the very few numbers upon which he must act. They should be presented as positive and negative exceptions. Positive exceptions will be those that should prompt reinforcement of good behavior, and negative exceptions will be those on which problem-solving actions should be based. Both positive and negative exceptions will be determined by the use of statistical procedures.

CREATING CULTURES OF QUALITY THOUGHT

What is it then that management can do to improve the quality of thought within the business and thereby improve its competitive position? Improving the quality of thought in the firm will determine the long-term viability of the business.

First, senior executives must understand, as Tom Watson did, that it is they and their ability to think well that set a model for the rest of the organization. If decision making is lacking in rationality at lower levels, it is probably just as lacking at senior levels. Senior executives must improve their decision making by the use of statistical procedures. This means not just having a lot of numbers to support a decision, but understanding them statistically.

Second, a program of education must be established throughout the firm so that every manager is taught how to look at his or her own numbers through the use of statistical methods. Every new employee hired should be taught the use of control charts so that he or she can understand them. These control charts should be available to every worker in every location of the organization, and should reflect every key performance variable. When managers walk through the manufacturing section of a plant or other facility where the work is done, they should stop and talk to individual workers. Ask them how they know how well they are doing. Where are their scores posted for them to see and study? Do they understand the trends in their own performance or the performance of their team? Do they understand the variability in their performance, what figures represent statistical control for the performance? There is nothing terribly difficult about promoting this awareness in every employee. The workers are perfectly capable of understanding if management will make the information available to them and train them in its use. This is the first step toward self-management and a very long step toward improving motivation and quality.

Third, management must help the data-processing professionals understand what is really important. Managers and employees need to see their scores on a regular time basis (daily at the operating level, no less than weekly above that); they need to see, not just today's performance, which is meaningless, but its trend in relation to previous performance; they need to see its statistical relationship to other data; and they need to see it presented graphically.

Fourth, management must accept greater responsibility for the educational system which prepares employees for the work force. I propose that every business in America adopt a school, if it is a large business (or a class if it is small) and assist that school in the education process. The business can assist by involving children for some number of hours each week so that the students can see why a mathematical concept is useful at work, or why relationships between people are important, or how a chemical process is applied in manufacturing. Children need early exposure to the real world and a real-world understanding of the application of knowledge. Teachers in the isolation of school cannot provide this. The business should loan professionals to the school to teach math, chemistry, and other relevant courses both to relieve the overburdened teachers and to provide variety and stimulation for the children. A benefit that may be as great could be that the professionals themselves will be stimulated by the refreshing curiosity and honesty of the young mind.

EIGHT

The Intimacy Principle

Intimacy is that invisible thread between the inner person, his manager, and the organization they serve. It is intimacy that permits trust, sacrifice, and loyalty.

Harold Little observed life as supervisor of textile finishing in a plant belonging to Mason Mills[1] in a small town in South Carolina. He had worked in the plant for about twenty years. His father had worked there before him. His brother also worked in a similar plant belonging to Mason Mills. When Harold began working for Mason, almost everyone who worked in the plant lived in the town. Only the plant manager had been brought in from another location and he, too, became a part of the community and remained there for the following twelve years. Mr. Mason, president, chairman, and principal owner, visited the mill almost every week. He and his family (the actual division of ownership was never made public) owned five small plants within fifty miles of each other. Mr. Mason knew the majority of his employees by their first name and made a point of meeting any new employee. Any decision regarding promotions, raises, or other significant personnel matters always involved Mr. Mason. This had not been a problem because there was a general and sincere belief that he dealt justly with people. The management style of this company could undoubtedly be labeled paternalism; however, it was paternalism of a mutually agreeable variety.

When Harold came to work for Mason, events at the mill were interwoven with events in the community. This mill was the primary business of the town. If there was a conflict between individuals within the plant, it was prime subject for gossip in the town. On the other hand, if someone had a personal problem, a marriage, a new baby, a visit by a distant relative, all of these events were cause for conversation, celebration, or grief within the company. It was understood that the plant manager and his secretary were responsible for orchestrating the in-plant response to these personal events. A wedding or new baby always resulted in a cake in the cafeteria during break.

There was one moment in Harold's life that he would always remember as the event most symbolic of the relationship between his company and his personal life. About ten years ago his wife had lost a baby at birth. They had only one other child, a girl, and there had been much discussion about the pregnancy and Harold's desire for a boy this time around. Harold had been at the hospital until about two o'clock the night of the ill-fated birth. He came to work the next morning at the usual hour. Somehow, by the time shift began that morning, word had gotten back to the plant regarding the unfortunate outcome of the labor. The plant manager walked through the mill every morning to inspect the progress of work and to chat with his employees. On his rounds this morning he found Harold standing quietly in a corner of his department staring aimlessly into space. The plant manager walked over to Harold and put his arm around his shoulders. "Anything we can do, Harold, you just let me know. Take whatever time you need." Harold said nothing in reply.

The next morning there was a small church funeral at which the family gathered. It was a short and quiet affair. Harold's wife sat in a wheelchair, not yet recovered from labor. Harold and a dozen or so family members stood close by as the minister read from the Bible. As the ceremony was in progress, a car drove up. Mr. Mason, the plant manager, and two other managers to whom Harold reported all got out of the car, dressed in their best suits, and walked up to the gravesite. They stood in prayer until the ceremony was complete. They never said anything, they just returned to their car, and drove off. Harold never forgot that moment.

Mason Mills changed over the years. Mr. Mason's son assumed more control of the business, as had been expected. He seemed to be a bit more ambitious than the old man. The junior Mr. Mason was better educated and understood more about efficiency, marketing, and other management practices in which he felt his father had been negligent. Money was borrowed for new high-speed looms imported from Italy. Managers were sent to more training classes. The practice of rotating managers between plants was begun to give each manager greater exposure. The company also began to hire more managers from outside the company. Supposedly Mason had been so far behind in its development of management skills that this was the only way they could keep up with the competition.

At the same time, changes were taking place in the town. The South had become attractive for plant location by northern companies in diverse industries. A tire plant and a large brewery had been built in nearby towns. The days when everyone worked for Mason Mills were now gone. Young people might work for any one of a dozen better-paying industries or move out completely. Harold's loyalties were to the mill and he had little desire for change.

Harold's most difficult days at the mill began with the arrival of Wayne Gardner, who rode into town as the new plant manager determined to demonstrate his abilities. Wayne was in his middle thirties and had been recruited from another textile firm where he had been a department manager. He apparently had training and early experience in the financial end of the business. He had never had the responsibility of being plant manager before. Wayne had a mission and that mission was never fully shared with anyone, but it was sensed that this assignment held great opportunity. He was determined to succeed, and it quickly became clear that success was defined exclusively in terms of financial performance.

Wayne early established a pattern of meetings with his managers. Once a week they would review their numbers from the week before. Wayne would ask them to set a higher goal, almost independent of what the previous performance had been. If a manager's performance had declined, Wayne would lecture the group on the financial goals for the plant and how "we" were going to meet those goals because "we" could do it. There was something about these talks that was slightly reminiscent of old Vince Lombardi films, but not quite. The acting was not convincing.

Wayne's goal setting became more determined. The numbers became increasingly hard to attain. On the floor the employees began to feel the pressure. They sensed that their managers were being pushed and they in turn were feeling the heat. After about nine months this pressure entered a new phase. At first, twelve employees were laid off. Later twenty. And in two months another fifteen. The plant kept up its production, but not without significant strain. Supervisors were doing more hands-on work, workers were covering more looms per shift than they ever had before. Second-quality cloth increased. Morale decreased. Turnover and absenteeism increased. Costs decreased and income remained the same.

This was when Harold entered his own existential crisis. He had worked in the mill for almost twenty years. He had given a lot of his own personality, his life, to this company. It had been good to him and he had no complaints. But it wasn't the same company anymore. The closeness was gone. People weren't concerned about people anymore. They were concerned about things: goals, costs, first quality or second quality, this piece of equipment or that, and how it all made the individual manager look in someone's eyes. Harold didn't feel a part of that. His spirit wasn't connected to what was going on in the mill anymore. He wasn't sure whether there wasn't something terribly wrong with him. Maybe he was getting old. But he knew that he still wanted to work, he wanted to be connected, involved, and excited. It was these new rules that he wasn't sure he could learn; or did he want to?

Harold was suffering the loss of intimacy. He had belonged to a community of people who cared about each other. The mill had been a "good neighborhood," a good place to live. Employees had been motivated and loyal. Employees had spoken proudly of "their mill." A new culture was taking shape at Mason Mills. It was a culture driven by numbers, financial priorities, images, and ambitions. People began to take sides for and against. Employees did not speak as openly to supervisors. And eventually, the word was spoken in the town, the word that had been considered subversive, almost un-Godly: union.

The transformation of Mason Mills and its redefinition of the relationship between the individual and firm is one which has taken place in thousands of similar companies. They go through a life cycle. There is the early period of dominance by a personality—Mr. Mason, the "old man," whose values and spirit define the culture of the organization and the relationship that employees have to the firm. Then there is the efficiency period when the management of the firm is assumed by allegedly more professional managers who attack the informal ways in which things got done before, increase the reliance on procedure, form, and technology. This phase almost always is accompanied by an identity crisis, a loss of intimacy between the individual and the organization. Then, it is hoped, the firm will enter an age of maturity in which it is able to reach a balance between efficient procedure and personal concern and involvement. As individual companies often go through these transitions, it may well be that the larger cycles of management on a national or even global scale also are passing through similar transitions.

THE INTIMATE FUNCTION OF THE CORPORATION

We are entering an age in which the functions and responsibilities of the corporation and its managers are being challenged.[2] This challenge is based, properly, on the recognition that we, as a society, are not adequately meeting human needs when it is within our capacity to do so. Some will seek to limit and control the corporation and assume certain of its current functions with tax-funded services. I believe the result of that challenge will not be a restriction on the functions of the corporation, but rather will result in an expansion of the expectations and responsibilities placed on the business enterprise. This expansion will occur for the simple reason that the corporate unit and its system of functioning have proved to be the most effective institution for the assignment of resources devised by our society or any other. Despite its occasional excesses and injustices, there is no better method for accomplishing the tasks of producing goods and services, the components of wealth.

In addition to its fundamental task of producing goods and services within the bounds of law and good citizenship, the corporate institution will assume increasing responsibility for the education, development, and care of its individual members. This shift, already well in progress, will result in a more intimate relationship, a closer bond between the individual and the corporation. The need to belong to a group of significance, the need to be cared for, and the need to feel that one is making a worthy contribution must be fulfilled within the relationship between the business and individual. The corporation demands too much of the individual's time and energies not to fulfill this basic psychological need. Indeed, its fulfillment will become even more necessary as the options increase, and as the work becomes increasingly cerebral and creative and less repetitive.

The need for intimacy is among the most fundamental of human concerns. Intimacy is the ability to share oneself in a thorough and trusting manner and to receive, in return, sincere appreciation and concern for one's personal interests. Intimacy may also be defined as the ability to give and receive love. Intimacy exists in the most healthy relationships between individuals and organizations. Intimacy produces the more sought-after commodities of trust, dedication, and sacrifice.

Future historians may be able to divide the development of the corporation and its human relations into three distinct stages: preindustrial family-centered, industrial age adversarial, and information age community.

PREINDUSTRIAL FAMILY-CENTERED

The preindustrial business was centered on a craft or skill. The management of finances, sales, and administration was subordinate to the primary task that involved the majority of the participants. The primary task was the skillful crafting of furniture, shoes, or other product with which the worker could identify upon completion. The product could be worn, used by one's friends and neighbors, and perhaps even autographed or initialed, assuring that one had "made one's mark." The craft was generally passed on by the senior craftsman to his apprentices, commonly members of his own family. The craftsman was respected for his skill and was the center of the enterprise. He and his apprentices formed a family unit whose interests were inextricably interwoven. The respect due the senior craftsman also honored the apprentices.

The intimate relationships between members of the preindustrial business were not unlike the intimacy found on the family farm. The members of the unit worked together in close company, performing tasks that were interdependent, passing on skills as from father to son, and sharing in the social as well as the financial success of the enterprise. At a time in American history when the family, church, and community were all relatively strong, the individual also benefited from the close human bonds of the workplace.

Mason Mills and many other industries isolated in an otherwise agrarian environment carried the paternalistic style of the preindustrial family-centered business culture, its benefits and its tyrannies well into this century. The forces of mobility, competition, and technology are eliminating these last holdouts of industrial intimacy.

INDUSTRIAL AGE ADVERSARIAL

The Industrial Revolution and the society it created in the northern and eastern United States were founded on entirely different assumptions than those which preceded it. In the preindustrial age, the success of a business was based on the skills of its craftsmen and their ability to work as a cohesive unit. In the new manufacturing industries, human competence was not viewed as the critical dimension in the success of the enterprise. Capital, equipment, process, and product were the determinants of success. The individual was easily replaced and the processes were increasingly designed to be worker independent. The less skill required on the part of any individual, the better. The more easily the production process could be faithfully replicated, the less likely it would be subject to compromise by the untrustworthy intentions of the worker.

Workers were almost viewed as a necessary annoyance: the least predictable and controllable elements in the creation of this new efficiency. Frederick Taylor's method of reducing the task to its most fundamental elements was consistent with the philosophy that workers only did simple and definable tasks and it was those tasks which must be managed, not the person himself. There were large numbers of workers "doing" and a few managers "thinking and deciding." The management of managers was not yet an issue because they were well rewarded as opposed to their subordinates, the workers, and they exercised unchallenged authority.

This industrial enterprise offered little in the way of intimacy between the organization and the individual. The enterprise was huge and the individual small. The enterprise wielded enormous power and the individual none. The enterprise had no dependence on the individual worker, and the worker was entirely dependent on the will of the enterprise. Intimacy cannot exist without some measure of equality; if not equality in numbers, then equality of spirit. Intimacy is reinforced by reciprocity. One must be able to give and receive, and neither, in any measure, can substitute for the absence of the other.

The creation of the union movement and the establishment of the adversarial norm between management and labor were natural and necessary outgrowths of the lack of intimacy. The union fulfilled the need to belong to a group of individuals who shared a mutual concern and demonstrated a caring attitude, testifying to the self-worth of each member. Union membership fulfilled safety, security, and social needs. The company denigrated the worth of the individual through its system of production. The union enabled the worker to feel strong and dignified. The stronger the statement of one, the stronger the statement of the other and the more divergent their positions and adversarial their relations. The consumption of human energy required to maintain this adversary position has contributed to the primary inefficiency in our industrial system that has allowed world competition to advance on the United States. This adversarial relationship has been modified under the pressures of competition, which have created a more pressing mutual concern, economic survival. However, most corporations have not begun to conceive of how they will eliminate the need for an adversarial relationship in good times as well as bad.

THE INFORMATION AGE COMMUNITY

The preindustrial business enterprise fulfilled needs for intimacy at a time when the family, church, and community met the needs of the individual more adequately than they do today. We live in a more fragmented society with fewer institutions meeting the needs for human bonding. The human condition has not so dramatically altered that the needs for belonging and caring are significantly diminished. I would not be so foolish as to propose that the corporate entity makes it its business to fulfill those needs out of a motive of pure benevolence. On the contrary, the motive to create intimacy within the corporation will be practical self-interest: It will be good business.

CREATIVE COMMUNITIES

The intimacy that I am proposing will not be based on the giving of material benefits, corporate-welfare social work, or the creation of states of dependence between person and firm. The intimacy will be based on mutual respect, independence, and mutual concerns. It will be the intimacy of a mature marriage—neither burdensome nor stifling.

The first need of the corporation that will propel this relationship will be to maximize the production of the human capital in which it has invested. Increasingly the corporation will succeed, not because of the performance of its equipment, but as a result of the creativity of its people. It will be the primary responsibility of the manager to create those environments in which the individual is able to maximize his or her personal talents and abilities. The corporation is trading in the output of human energy. The creation and management of that energy will be the primary test of the manager's ability.

The process of creativity and the release of human energy are closely linked to the concept of intimacy. Creativity is not maximized when the individual sits silently in the corner dreaming of wondrous new technologies, although there may be moments of such behavior. Creativity is more commonly fostered when small groups of similarly talented individuals freely exchange ideas in the total absence of judgment or fear of condemnation. The friendly, informal chatting about ideas in which one has a genuine interest and enthusiasm is the forum in which creative energy is released and stimulated. For this reason, there is a history of communities of creative persons that have emerged to promote talent and energy. The artistic and literary communities of Paris in the last century, the Greenwich Village communities of the decades past, and the writer-actor producer communities of California and New York all existed then and do now because of the necessary human dynamics of creativity. Without planning or deliberation, persons of similar talents have congregated to meet their needs for stimulation, to share common ideas, and to seek the appreciation of their peers. It is precisely the same dynamic that the corporation must engineer.

An examination of those corporate settings that have successfully promoted innovation and creativity will reveal cultures in which individuals are comfortable sharing their ideas without fear. Creative communities exist within small pockets of corporations today. They are, however, more likely to flourish within the small entrepreneurial firm. The small company is more apt to be one in which individuals of similar talents are able to share ideas and to brainstorm openly. It is for this reason that small entrepreneurial firms have led in technological innovation. Large corporations with their procedures, politics, and often impersonal treatment of the individual are less likely to promote the human environment in which creativity is stimulated.

It requires no small shift in orientation on the part of most managers to recognize that the process of creativity, rather than something in the preserve of the "odd," is the primary source of profit to the corporation. Our image is that profit is produced by mindless dedication to the running of the machine or to the hard-nosed financial decision makers, who have the toughness to "cut out the fat" from the meat of the business. While these characters may still have their place they will become increasingly subordinate to individuals who are able to design the most sophisticated microprocessor, imagine the applications and workings of software that will be needed in the office or home of the future, or create the product marketing strategy with appeal to a crosscultural population. These are all tasks requiring thought and creativity that will thrive in a culture of intimacy and that would be crushed in a culture of intimidation and conformity. The corporation will have to decide where its self-interests lie.

The impact of women upon the corporation has yet to be felt in any significant way. As women have entered the work force, their response has been more to adapt to the style requirements of the institution than to force a change of style upon the institution. Women have yet to legitimize a more "feminine" style of management. Those women who have entered the ranks of management, although there are exceptions, have had a tendency to adapt to the style of management of their corporations. Unfortunately, that style is often of the macho, quick-draw variety which is destined to extinction. If women continue to forsake the qualities in which they are superior, the same qualities the corporation needs most to incorporate into its future culture, it may truly be said that while women may have won the job, men have won the battle of the sexes, and we have all lost the war. It is more likely that as the numbers of women increase in the ranks of corporate managers, their presence will be characterized less by the abandonment of feminine qualities and more by the expansion and development of those qualities within the unified culture of the organization.

This is an age of integration. Men, conditioned by the requirements of military discipline and by the numbing toil of fields and factories, have learned over the centuries to suppress emotion and expression. Women, conditioned by centuries of mothering, have superior experience in the realm of caring and intimacy. The latter qualities are the ones toward which our corporate cultures must move, and the integration of women into these cultures should be viewed not merely as calling upon an additional pool of similar talent, and surely not as an exercise in compliance to imposed standards, but as an enrichment of the repertoire and talents of the human capital of corporations.

American business is not likely to adopt Japan's pattern of lifetime employment as has been so much discussed. Neither will we witness the unquestioning dedication of employees to their corporation as is common in Japan. We are no more likely to adopt these patterns than we would the pattern of Japanese domestic life in which the extended family and paternal superiority are dominant. These relationships are contrary to the individualism and dedication to equality that are such strong characteristics of the American culture and among its primary strengths. As American business matures in its understanding of the role of the individual, his needs, the involvement, respect, and self-esteem that are so critical to his creative performance, a new intimacy will develop.

NINE

The Integrity Principle

Leadership requires followership and following is an act of trust, faith in the course of the leader, and that faith can be generated only if leaders act with integrity.

In an age in which subordinates cannot be required to follow, an age in which the individual will be bound to no institution, an age in which the ability to lead people collectively in creative pursuit will be the most sought-after talent, the first and highest requirement of a leader will be integrity. Of all the principles of the new leadership it is integrity with which there can be no compromise. Consensus may be incomplete. Purpose at times may be unclear and shifting. Excellence will always be relative. Consequences will be only somewhat related to performance. However, integrity must be the most certain, the least subject to doubt, of the qualities of the new leader. The same integrity must become the bedrock of the new corporate culture.

Integrity is honesty and the consistent, responsible pursuit of a stated course of action. The person or organization that has integrity can be trusted. From trust comes security, the individual's knowledge of how the world around will respond to his actions.

There can be no leadership without integrity. Leadership requires followership, and following is an act of trust, of faith in the course of the leader. Integrity is desirable because it is a compenent of power, the power to create and mobilize human energy, to get things done through people. James MacGregor Burns has defined leadership as "exercised when persons with certain motives and purposes mobilize, in competition or conflict with others, institutional, political, psychological, and other resources so as to arouse, engage, and satisfy the motives of followers."[1] Leadership occurs when the motives of the followers are satisfied. The genius of leadership is the mobilization of human energy in pursuit of goals held by the followers, and this may be accomplished only under the condition of trust between leader and followers.

WHAT MANAGERS RESPECT

A survey conducted by the American Management Association on the subject of managerial values and expectations asked approximately 1,500 managers and executives to identify the qualities they admired most in their subordinates, colleagues, and superiors. The respondents reported by listing different traits, 225 of them. The researchers distilled these traits into what they felt were fifteen distinct categories. The following is a list of those fifteen in alphabetical order.[2]

1. Broadmindedness (open-minded, flexible, receptive)
2. Competence (capable, productive, efficient, thorough)
3. Cooperativeness (friendly, team player, available, responsive)
4. Dependability (reliability, conscientious, predictable)
5. Determination (industrious, hard-working, motivated)
6. Fairness (objective, consistent, democratic)
7. Imagination (creative, innovative, curious)
8. Integrity (truthful, trustworthy, has character, has conviction)
9. Intelligence (bright, thoughtful, logical)
10. Leadership (inspiring, decisive, provides direction)
11. Loyalty (has a commitment to me, the company, or policies)
12. Maturity (experienced, wise, well grounded, has depth)
13. Straightforwardness (direct, candid, forthright)
14. Sensitivity (appreciation, concerned, aware, respectful)
15. Supportiveness (understanding, empathetic, helpful)

The respondents were asked to identify the value they admired most in subordinates, colleagues, and superiors separately. Integrity was the highest-rated quality for all three. For superiors, an identical 24 percent rated integrity first, with leadership and competency following, for peers, cooperation and next, competency; and for subordinates, determination, then competency.

In the same survey, the participants were also asked to check six values in a list of eighteen they considered to be most important in themselves and others. The two that headed the list were "responsible" (88 percent) and "honest" (87.7 percent). These two traits were mentioned 20 percent more often than the next choice, "capable," which was followed by "imaginative" and "logical."

The Cox Report on the American Corporation,[3] perhaps the most comprehensive survey of the attitudes and beliefs of American managers, asked participants to rate the impact of different qualities or abilities on career advancement within their corporations. The quality of "honesty" received by far the highest rating. "Honesty" was rated as having a "very positive" impact by 75.2 percent of the participants; "good judgment" by 62.1 percent; and "knowing how to set priorities and stick with them" by 58.1 percent.

It is clear from these surveys that managers require integrity from their superiors, peers, and subordinates. One does not make it in management today, and will be less likely to do so in the future, if one lacks integrity. The view of management from within is so entirely different from that portrayed in the pop culture on television and in the movies that it would appear there are two different species. The often-portrayed media image of the executive is likely to be of a deceitful, selfish, manipulative polluter of the environment and exploiter of the downtrodden, caught and chastised by Jane Fonda in all her self-righteous outrage. Certainly there are executives and managers lacking in integrity and honesty. However, it is a safe prediction that the percentage of such persons found in the executive suite is less than that which is common to the population at large, which is due, if for no other reason, to the rigorous selection process required to reserve a seat in the executive suite.

The executive of the future is likely to be of higher integrity than the executive of today because of the changing nature of power within the corporation. In days past, the manager may have been able to get the job done by wielding authoritative power. Managers have risen through the ranks by imposing their will and determination on their subordinates. The adversarial culture of much of American industry reinforced the use of authoritarian power. As recently as 1980 I heard a senior executive of a U.S. automobile manufacturing firm say, regarding the layoffs of auto workers, "Now we've got the bastards where we want them." Shortly thereafter, the "bastards" included a'large number of managers of reasonably high rank as the company laid off management in equal proportion to labor. Within a few short years the recognition that labor and management have more interests in common than in opposition has penetrated the psyche of the majority of U.S. managers.

THE IMPERATIVE OF TRUST

The executive of the future will be unable to rise through his use of force. He will have too little force in the traditional sense at his disposal. What he will have to call upon will be the force of his personality and his ability to draw out, stimulate, guide, and reinforce the behavior needed to achieve the mutually held purpose of both manager and employee. In other words, the manager of the future will have to be more the leader and less the administrator.

Robert Tannenbaum and Warren H. Schmidt have defined what they term a continuum of leadership behavior.[4] To the left of this continuum is boss-centered leadership, and to the right, subordinate-centered leadership (see Figure 1). They have more recently

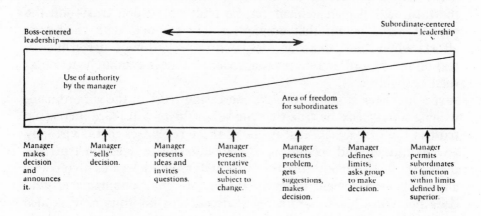

Boss-centered leadership ———————————→ Subordinate-centered leadership

Use of authority by the manager

Area of freedom for subordinates

| Manager makes decision and announces it. | Manager "sells" decision. | Manager presents ideas and invites questions. | Manager presents tentative decision subject to change. | Manager presents problem, gets suggestions, makes decision. | Manager defines limits; asks group to make decision. | Manager permits subordinates to function within limits defined by superior. |

redefined the ends of the continuum as "manager power and influence," on the left, and "nonmanager power and influence," on the right. Tannenbaum and Schmidt encourage managers to place their leadership style at a point on the continuum after considering a number of variables such as the type of organization, effectiveness of the group, and so on. Points on the continuum to the right imply increasing levels of trust and reliance on the subordinate. The manager who "makes the decision and announces it" quite obviously has a high degree of trust in his own decision-making ability and substantially less in his subordinates. The manager who "permits subordinates to function within limits defined by the superior" places more trust in the ability and integrity of the subordinates.

The trend in management is clearly toward the right of the continuum; that is, toward placing increasingly high levels of trust in subordinates. The views that the less management is the best management, that the productivity problem is a problem of management productivity, and that there are excessive numbers and levels of management within our corporations are becoming widely held. There is a resurgence of the use of "self-managed work teams" or of "semiautonomous work groups" as a means of thinning the layers of management and utilizing the higher abilities of the work force which have been suppressed in the past. The concept of self-management may well become the dominant theme of the organizations of the future. Self-management can be built only upon trust—on the part of management that employees will respond with their best efforts when the systems are designed to reward good performance, and on the part of employees that management is genuinely acting in their best interests.

If a manager is going to place increasing trust in the subordinate, it must necessarily be true that the subordinate will place increasing trust in the manager. Trust is one of those responses that is virtually always mutual and reciprocal. If the subordinate does not trust the manager, it is unlikely that the latter will trust, delegate, involve, or allow self-management to be the dominant style. The manager who does not trust his subordinates is derelict in his duty. He is also derelict in his duty if he has created a team of subordinates in whom he cannot place his trust.

It is the manager's ability to act with integrity and to be viewed by his subordinates as possessing integrity that permits the movement toward greater autonomy, self-management, and efficiency.

BEHAVING WITH INTEGRITY

How then does a manager who communicates integrity to his subordinates behave? It is certainly worth examining what a manager actually does. However, this examination is not intended to imply that one need merely "know" what to do as one might need to know how to write a clear objective. While I examine in the following section some of the mechanisms that result in integrity, I recognize that our ability to manage the values of subordinates is limited. The best we can do is act with integrity ourselves, create a culture in which integrity is a primary value, and select for promotion only those managers who have demonstrated high integrity.

SHORT-TERM SACRIFICE/LONG-TERM GAIN

Managers who demonstrate integrity know the larger purpose of their organization and are focused on long-term objectives. They know that those objectives are achieved through the accomplishment of hundreds of short-term goals, but they are willing to sacrifice the achievement of a short-term goal if in their view it detracts from the larger purpose (often the integrity) of the organization. Short-term/long-term decisions are made in many organizations each month or quarter, and center on the companies' short-term financial objectives. It is not at all uncommon for the short-term financial objectives of a firm to be met to the detriment of long-term performance. Any fool can meet a profit objective by cutting today's costs. Unfortunately, the sacrifice that is made in the cost cutting often undermines those functions (research and development or training) that have most to do with the ability of the firm to perform in the long term. The short-term perspective may also be manifested by the manager shipping a product that he knows to be of inadequate quality, realizing the revenue on his books, hoping that the customer will let it pass, but jeopardizing the business in the long run by creating an impression of shabby quality in the eyes of the customer.

While there are times when it is proper to make short-term decisions, a pattern of this behavior is quickly perceived by employees, and it properly causes them to understand that the priority of management is not the achievement of any higher goal or purpose for the firm, but the realization of short-term numbers. The same behavior should then be expected of subordinates.

FOLLOW-THROUGH

Managers who are trusted do what they say they will do. They are consistent in their talk and action. There is an unfortunate tendency among many managers to motivate and manage through their verbal behavior alone: management by speaking. They have some misperceived notion of "the motivator" as someone who delivers motivating words in a motivating fashion. They have watched too many Vince Lombardi-George Allen films and believe it was convincing words that produced motivation and winning teams. True only for very short moments. The value of words disappears quickly. It is the consistency of the manager's own behavior with his own words that has more long-term impact.

It is in fashion these days to promote better-quality production. Managers are posting signs encouraging workers to spot defects and "do it right the first time." However, employees are watching management carefully to ascertain where the true priorities lie. A firm recently developed a new product and invested a great deal of money and its reputation on the new product. The chief executive officer had announced to company stockholders the forthcoming introduction of the new product. The CEO placed enormous pressure on the engineering team to get the item into production by the date the CEO had promised. The engineers were not on schedule. They were working twelve-hour days, seven days a week, but were encountering technical difficulties that had to be overcome if the product was to perform as advertised. The CEO exhorted them, telling them that they could, must, and would do it. The product was finished on schedule despite warnings by the engineers that it had been inadequately tested. After several hundred of the units had been delivered, the defects became apparent. Lawsuits followed and all the units were recalled for modification. The CEO fired the team of five engineers that had been responsible for the product's development. All of this from a CEO who spoke proudly of the importance of quality and integrity.

PRIORITY OF PRODUCT OR SERVICE

The love of and devotion to product or service leads to integrity. The manager who has a genuine love for automobiles is more likely to sell finer automobiles than the manager who is simply interested in making money. I used to own a Alfa Romeo Spider sports car. There was only one place in Atlanta where any true aficionado would consider having an Alfa serviced. Dozens of service centers claimed they could tune and service an Alfa, but there was only one who loved them. Paul Spruell raced Alfas, collected them, loved them, and knew them better than the factory that built them. He would take time with each customer to discuss what he had done in servicing his car, which often went beyond what the customer thought he needed, because Paul knew what the car needed. He would replace small, round rubber gaskets between the head and cylinder block with new ones because these were superior to those used by the factory which would often fail. Paul would look at the car as he spoke about its inner workings the way a doctor looks at a patient to whom he relates a diagnosis. I doubt that customers often fully understood what Paul was talking about, but that didn't matter. They knew that he did and they knew that he cared about their car as they did, and for this they were happy to pay.

The manager with integrity is devoted to his product or service, and this is the best assurance of quality. If this same devotion can be communicated by all employees there will be no quality problems in American industry.

THE STRENGTH TO RESPECT

The manager who can be trusted, who possesses integrity, will almost always tend to make positive assumptions about others. The psychological mechanism of projection is at work here. We have a tendency to project feelings about ourselves onto others. If we feel inadequate, disappointed with ourselves, or guilty about some action, we are likely to strike out at others as though they were the cause of these feelings. This mechanism works in positive situations as well. The person who is honest, who is certain of his or her trustworthiness is more likely to see those qualities in others. Rather than assuming that people are devious such a person will assume that they may be trusted.

To be able to display respect and appreciation for the positive qualities of others is an indication of one's respect for oneself. Others respond to this behavior intuitively. We intuitively trust the person who has the good judgment to place trust in us. Because we perceive that the other person has high expectations of us, we act to fulfill those expectations. A cycle of trusting and trustworthy behavior is established by the manager who has the strength, the security, the self-respect that allow him to behave in a trusting way toward others. This is the manager who is able to listen sincerely to the ideas and concerns of others. This is the manager who does not need to take credit for each success, but feels most free in passing that credit on to his subordinates. This is the manager who does not require to know every detail of a subordinate's business, because he assumes that the subordinate is capable. This is the manager who does not punish poor performance on the assumption that the individual didn't try hard enough, but problem-solves with that individual to help him on the assumption that the person would perform if he could. This is the manager who displays integrity.

THE LAW OR THE SPIRIT?

We live in a society in which the pursuit of legal posture has become confused with the pursuit of just action. In many corporations the lawyers have become the high priests of right and wrong. Lawyers, with their training in the adversarial tradition, technical distinctions, and tactics, are generally no better suited than anyone else to make decisions about right and wrong. Because executives have come to rely upon lawyers for guidance in matters of conduct and ethical judgment, too often they have made decisions based on legal technicality rather than on their own judgment. Often the spirit of the matter is clear if the manager would only allow himself to act on it.

Several years ago there was a series of three airplane accidents. One accident was the Air Florida crash at Washington National Airport. The second was in Boston when the plane skidded off the runway and landed in the bay. The third was in Tokyo when a JAL (Japan Air Lines) plane crashed. In the JAL crash, the company had apparently had knowledge of some emotional problem on the part of the pilot. In the two U.S. crashes, the attorneys arrived on the scene before all the bodies were removed from the wreckage. It will undoubtedly be years, and after thousands of man-hours of expensive work, before all the litigation is settled in these two crashes. There was no lawsuit in the Tokyo crash. There are Japanese attorneys and litigation does occur in Japan. However, in this case, the chairman of

JAL, recognizing the company's responsibility to the victims, personally visited the home of each family, prayed with the family at the family altar, and agreed upon a settlement with the family.

The chairman of JAL did not act on legal technicality to gain legal advantage. He acted on his knowledge of what was right. Litigation is expensive and is essentiallly nonproductive. No new wealth is produced by the action of attorneys. The diversion of funds and human energy to legal activity detracts from society's ability to meet human needs. The sooner we can shift the focus of our actions away from legal technicalities toward actions guided by the true spirit of ethical conduct, the sooner we will add to the productive energies of our organizations.

THE CREATION OF INTEGRITY

Why then do some possess this quality of integrity while others do not? Where or by whom is this integrity created?

It is my experience and the experience of other observers that managers who inspire devotion have a dedication to a higher, sometimes mysterious, perhaps spiritual purpose. They believe in a cause, a reason, and a set of truths beyond their control and to which everything else must conform. These beliefs may be in God or religion, but it is always in a superior force or truth. It is the adherence to these beliefs and the mission to carry them forward that provides an internal security that allows them to behave with integrity. Their beliefs provide them with a sense of special significance, which is the key to their leadership. They know that they are not merely serving themselves, a goal for which they know little is worth sacrificing, but they are serving their cause, mission, or faith, for which great sacrifices are justified. Employees have an unspoken sensitivity to this spiritual significance and respond in a way that results in meaning within their own lives.

O. A. Ohmann has referred to these higher values as "skyhooks."[5] "In my studies of exceptional executives I had found a mystery not easily explained by rational elements. These men, too, were hanging on skyhooks of their own—hidden and secret missions which went way beyond their corporate business objectives. Sometimes the mission was a 'nutsy' one. Often it had long roots back in the executive's childhood and was emotional, intuitive, beyond rationality, selfless—but it stuck." "Many great executives I have known have something deep inside that supports them; something they trust when the going gets tough; something ultimate; something personal; something beyond reason—in short, a deep-rooted skyhook which brings them calm and confidence when they stand alone."

It is the presence of such "skyhooks" that permit the manager to take risks and do what he or she knows to be right rather than what is expedient. It is this faith which cushions the short-term sacrifices, losses, and humiliations which are inevitable acts in the play of an executive's career. It is these reference points against which all significant decisions are judged and determined. And this process produces a consistency and a predictability that can be trusted by others.

While interviewing executives, I have asked them to describe the person or persons who have had the greatest influence on the development of their own management style. The best executives rather consistently point to powerful role models from whom they learned and to whom they feel they owe their success. When asked to describe these models or mentors, they almost invariably describe their character, their trustworthiness, their dedication. Their mentors took an interest in the development of their subordinates. They demonstrated true caring and concern. They took the time to help and assist and teach. They were not so preoccupied with immediate business that they failed to address the needs of their subordinates. And they, too, believed in something.

What a noble service was provided by these mentors. What higher achievement by a manager can there be than to leave to posterity others who have adopted his spirit of integrity and purpose? If only every manager could be aware of his or her potential influence on future generations if he or she took the time to nurture others as these models have.

Integrity is contagious. As they do with most cultural traits, managers have learned to adopt what they feel are the normative values of the organization. Managers possessing integrity most often grew up in homes and communities and worked for companies that placed a high priority on doing what was right rather than what appeared to be of most immediate benefit. They were conditioned by a culture that valued integrity as a priority for its own sake. Perhaps the most important management-development task that our corporations face is to create a cultural learning process that teaches young managers to act on superior belief systems, to do that which they know to be right, according to a higher standard than what seems most expedient.

The response to higher standards implies sacrifice. Sacrifice of short-term appearances, numbers, or gain. However, there is a great mystery to genuine sacrifice. When we sacrifice for a noble cause, strangely, we find there has been no sacrifice. We become more worthy having made the sacrifice. And it is not long before that achievement produces the most attractive return on investment. For the manager who is able to respond with integrity will inspire confidence, performance, and dedication, the stuff of which success is made.

PART TWO

Managing Change

The following four chapters are intended as a guide to a process for managing change within a corporation's culture. Changing the culture of a corporation is no small task and requires a number of years of persistent and coordinated effort. To be successful, a change process should include both strategy and tactics. Among the strategic considerations are the definition of the current culture and the desired future culture. These definitions must be based on an evaluation of the major sources of influence on the culture, both internal and external.

Chapter 10 offers a series of indicators for the presence of cultural traits, both the primary values that are described in Part I, and the secondary values, which will vary depending on business circumstance. Chapter 11 provides a method for analyzing the influences on the culture: "who we are and how we are organized" (internal factors) and the "external environment." It is these forces which must be considered when attempting to define the ideal culture desired in the future.

Chapter 12 provides some guidelines for planning the tactics required to get the change process moving after the desired culture has been defined. Chapter 13 offers guidance as to how to make that change stick once the process is in motion.

TEN

Strategy: Defining the Culture

> Corporations will compete successfully only if they have
> achieved a culture that promotes the behavior necessary for
> competitive success. Every corporation owes its employees and
> stockholders a well-developed plan for the corporation's culture.

Changing the culture of an organization requires strategy. Strategy is a plan for development or change over a number of years and takes into account the interrelationships of functions, goals, and responsibilities within the organization and the effects of external influences. Few of our corporations have even begun to consider strategies for the development of their human environment or culture.[1] In the past the culture of the corporation was taken for granted. In the future it will be planned with as much care and deliberation as the financial, product, and market strategies of the firm. The business strategies of the corporation can succeed only if the human resources and performance are consistent with the corporation's business plan.[2] This chapter presents a model for developing a culture-change strategy.

Strategic planning is the responsibility of senior managers. Planning the culture that will maximize business performance is their responsibility. However, in developing such a plan it is wise to involve a broad base of managers at various levels of the organization. Commonly, the culture as perceived by senior executives bears little resemblance to the culture as perceived by middle managers, supervisors, or workers. It is best to involve all levels in a team process of defining the existing and the idealized cultures. It is also advisable that the definitions developed at lower levels of the organization be used as inputs into the planning of senior managers.

In planning and defining the culture of an organization there are six sets of definitions that must be developed by the teams. The first three concern the present and past; the last three concern the future:

How We Behave—Our Current Culture
  Who We Are and How We Are Organized
  The External Environment (Today and Yesterday)

How We Will Behave in The Future—Our Future Culture
  Who We Will Be and How We Will Be Organized
  The External Environment (Tomorrow)

Developing a vision of the type of culture desired by the organization must be done with full understanding of the business plan. Does the firm wish to remain in a traditional and stable manufacturing business, or does it seek to be a leader in new technologies? Will the firm's competition remain stable or will changing government regulations bring in new competitors? Or is the firm's primary strategy to service a stable market base and reduce costs? These different business strategies have significant implications for the development of the human culture.

Many corporations and even entire industries have been handicapped by their failure to plan the culture of their firms. Dozens of financial institutions, banks in particular, are faced with a dramatically changed business environment that demands new behavior from existing personnel, new organizations, incentives, and skills. When banks hired employees ten years ago, neither the banks nor the employees regarded sales and marketing skills as their concerns. Then banks were service and franchise oriented. The behavior and attitude of bank employees were in no way marketing or sales oriented, and were not competitive or entrepreneurial. Today banks find themselves in one of the most competitive and dynamic businesses in America, the financial services business, in which innovation, marketing, and sales are among the primary determinants of success. These banking corporations, as well as firms in dozens of other industries, will compete successfully only if they have achieved a culture that promotes behaviors that will lead to success in future competitive environments.[3] It is for this reason that every corporation owes its employees and stockholders a well-developed plan for the corporation's culture.

STRATEGIC CULTURE PLANNING MODEL

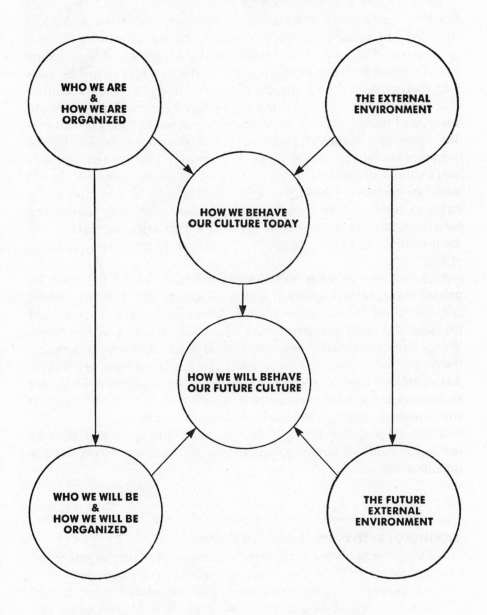

HOW WE BEHAVE—DEFINING OUR CULTURE

Managers need a framework and a language for articulating what features characterize their existing cultures and what behaviors they would like to see in the future. The current culture of the corporation is the sum of the habits of its members. These habits vary in some measure between units of the organization. The sales and marketing units of organizations are likely to have a culture that is somewhat different from the financial, research and development, and manufacturing segments of the organization. For this reason, planning teams should assess and develop a profile of the organization within each subunit. It is entirely possible that one segment should maintain a stable culture while another segment should undergo a virtual revolution. New technologies are forcing many firms to revolutionize their research, development, and engineering functions. At the same time it is possible that sales, marketing, administration, and even manufacturing may need to remain relatively stable.

Defining the existing and desired cultures should be done by guided teams in each segment and at each level. These teams should consider a number of factors in their definition process. They should consider the eight primary values described in Part I of this book. These values represent general cultural traits that are undergoing transition and will significantly affect the human culture of all businesses and all functions within them in the coming years. There are also secondary values: variable traits which may be considerations in some businesses or business units and not in others.

The following list of the primary values and questions may be used as a guide in defining the existing and desired cultures of the organization:

PRIMARY VALUES:

1. Purpose-Driven/Lacking Purpose

—Do the employees understand the mission of the organization and do they consider that mission to be of worth to society?

—Are management decisions made with consideration to the mission or purpose of the organization or do they tend to be primarily expedient?

2. Consensus/Command Decision Making

—Do managers agree in general as to which decisions are made in a command, consultative, or consensus manner?

—Are major decisions affecting the business unit made in a consensus manner?

—Do managers have the skills necessary to facilitate consensus decision making?

3. Excellence Ethic/Comfort-Satisfaction Dominant

—Are employees and managers engaged in a continual process of self-education and improvement?

—Is there a general understanding that each employee and small team is responsible for self-evaluation and accepting responsibility for change?

—Does the organization reward initiative (innovation)?

—Are managers generally satisfied or continually dissatisfied with today's performance?

4. Unity of Interest/Class-Distinct Interests

—When a business unit performs well, do all levels of the organization share in the rewards for that performance?

—Do managers make the assumption that employees are able to contribute meaningfully to the decision-making process?

—Are promotions and rewards based on personal competence along a continuum and not on status designations?

—Are employees working toward goals which they feel will contribute to the larger organization achieving *its* goals?

5. Performance-Based Rewards/Power- or Tenure-Based Rewards

—Are the strongest motivational forces rewards that may be achieved by performance or tenure?

—Is there a system for sharing financial gain based on superior performance at each level of the organization?

—When promotions are given, is the relationship between the individual's performance and his or her promotion clearly understood?

6. Empirical/Nonrational Decision Making

—Does each manager and employee team know the data for which they are responsible, have immediate access to those data, and plot the data over time?

—Are statistical procedures used in the analysis of data?

—When problems arise, are data gathered and analyzed in order to arrive at the desired course of action?

—Are data displayed and visible to employees throughout the work area?

7. Intimate Concern/Disposable Labor

—Does the organization demonstrate through its policies and actions that it is committed to the development of the individual within the firm?

—Are employees treated as significant stakeholders in the firm?

—Do individuals feel that their superiors are personally concerned with their well-being and that their needs will be responded to?

—Do managers place more emphasis on rewarding desirable behavior (positive control) or punishing undesirable behavior (negative control)?

8. Integrity Priority/Expedient Priority

—Does decision making include a priority concern for the long-term well-being of customers and employees?

—Do company communications convey the true purpose and motives for decisions?

—Do managers provide full and honest feedback to employees, and do employees feel comfortable providing full and frank feedback to their superiors?

SECONDARY VALUES: BUSINESS VARIABLE TRAITS:

1. Customer Focused/Product Focused

While entire companies tend to be oriented toward product (service) or customer, the tendency is even more pronounced within units of a business. Historically accounting firms have been service focused, not customer focused. The attention of managers and employees within the major accounting firms was on the technical aspects of the job. Being expert in a given area of accounting resulted in recognition and rewards. It was not in the nature of the business to be flexible in adapting to the needs of customers. On the contrary, it was the accounting firm that maintained the standards to which the customer had to conform. This orientation was for many years proper and successful. It is still proper for internal accounting, auditing, and other control organizations. For many years the major automobile manufacturers were not customer centered, they were product-manufacturing centered. This was based on the once-valid belief that they could determine future market preference rather than respond to existing preferences. Both the accounting firms and the automotive firms are now going through massive shifts in their cultural orientations. They are struggling to change the beliefs, thoughts, and behaviors of their members to become more responsive to the needs and opportunities presented by the customer population.

The marketplace in general is becoming increasingly competitive and, therefore, businesses will become increasingly customer focused rather than product focused. The following questions may be considered by planning teams who are defining the culture of the firm:

—Do managers discuss feedback from customers regularly with their subordinates?

—Are managers and employees more concerned about the functioning, production, and development of their product (or service) or are they more concerned with customers' use of their product or similar products?

—Are new products or services more likely to be the result of technical developments or as a response to customer requests or behavior?

2. Disciplined Control/Loose Control

Every organization must impose a measure of control if it is to function anywhere this side of chaos. Most managements agree that chaos is undesirable, although appearances might prove deceiving in this regard. The degree of control exerted and the tolerance for diversity are major factors affecting the human environment. An organization can commit the error of either too much discipline or too loose control. Where on the continuum you may wish to be is somewhat dependent on the nature of the business.

I recently had dealings with one international banking organization that was highly entrepreneurial. The managers were very freewheeling characters who had a high degree of freedom, and also were not prone to conforming to controls on lending practices. A number of incidences in which very large sums of money were lent only to be followed by the disappearance of the lendee convinced senior management that it was time to change the culture toward a more disciplined adherence to procedure.

Another bank, of the domestic variety, recently realized that its former franchise was being invaded by others in the financial services business and that its managers, so concerned about procedures and disciplines that they were scarcely aware that they actually "wanted" to lend money, were turning away customers with their rigidity. Both banks had evolved cultures that were once appropriate to their external environment; both were very successful, however, and both were struggling to change their culture to meet new business conditions.

Questions which may be asked regarding the business overall and specific business units include:

—Are procedures and control systems viewed as resulting in a slow response to customers or technology?

—Do employees communicate that adherence to a procedure or policy is more important than meeting customer needs?

—Are there unnecessary costs, risks, or lost opportunities that result from the absence of procedure or failure to follow procedures?

3. Entrepreneurial/Tried and True

The word "entrepreneurial" has become a term of assumed positive value. Indeed, the entrepreneurial spirit and behavior of the American business person are probably the strongest cultural driving forces in the American economy. However, it should not be assumed that every organization and every manager within subunits of an organization should be motivated and behave in an entrepreneurial manner. Some people and organizations have to stick to the tried and true, and not experiment or take risks with company assets. Cannon Mills has stuck to the towel, sheet, and pillowcase business for many years. New colors and designer sheets represented about the extent of its entrepreneurial behavior. Doing a few things better and in larger quantity than anyone else proved a highly successful strategy and culture for Cannon for many years. On the other hand, there are many examples of businesses succeeding because of their strategies of encouraging innovation and new business development. 3M, Proctor & Gamble, and Texas Instruments have built their businesses on product development, the creation of new markets, and technical innovation. Either an entrepreneurial or a tried-and-true strategy can be successful if it is based on a proper analysis of the marketplace. The human cultures to support these strategies are each extremely different.

—If an employee has an idea for product innovation, is he or she able to be involved in its development or is the idea turned over to others?

—Do managers focus more on sales increase, cost control, and efficiency, or do they focus more on product-market innovation and change?

—Have the products and services of the firm undergone rapid change over the past several years or have they remained stable?

4. Fast Decision Making/Slow Decision Making

Quick decision making has been a cultural value of the American manager. It is consistent with getting ahead quickly, with the need for quick decisions by the quarterback on the playing field, the commander on the battlefield, and the ticking of the clock on the quiz show. Without a doubt there are situations in which this is a justified value. The sales manager in the customer's office and the plant manager on the production line are often required to make quick decisions. When promoted to senior positions, these managers often bring their quick draw with them to the world of strategy. While quick decisions may still be valued, their benefits are decidedly less prominent. Japanese decision making, never accused of being too quick, has confronted the American management value for quick decision making. The Japanese take their time making decisions, are far more willing to let the matter rest, create involvement and consensus until the right decision is apparent. The nature of the business and the segment of the organization dictate the most appropriate tendency toward fast-deciding/slow-deciding strategy.

—Does decision making require so much time that opportunities for new business or reduced costs are lost?

—Do decisions get made so quickly that they are not understood by those who must carry them out, and do they frequently prove to have been unwise?

5. Short-Term Focus/Long-Term Focus

Managers think in different time frames. The planning–strategy-trained marketing specialist thinks in long time frames. The former plant manager who has spent his life concerned with performance over a period of three daily shifts in the plant has a short time focus. The appropriate time frame is less a function of the type of business than it is of the particular area of the business or the level of decision making. Every business must zero in on both long-term actions and on short-term ones. Different people and functions should have different perspectives. The marketing and research and development units of a business must be centered on the long term. If they are focused on today's customer or today's technology and methods, they are, by definition, not performing their function. On the other hand, the manufacturing and sales managers had best not be worrying about the changing demographics of target populations and future technologies, but should concern themselves with today's numbers, products, and customers.

It is common for managers at one level of the organization to be inappropriately concerned with performance on the wrong time scale. Division manufacturing managers are often responding to production numbers on a daily basis and by so doing they create increased fluctuation and variability in the manufacturing process. If they kept their noses out of daily performance and focused on the larger systems for which they are responsible, they would experience better day-to-day performance.

—Does each level of management have a progressively longer and more strategic perspective than the one below?

—Is some person or group of persons clearly responsible for the markets, products, technologies, and manufacturing processes that will be required in the three- to five-year time frame?

—Are operating managers in sales and production appropriately focused on the immediate performance for which they are responsible?

6. High Tech/Low Tech

One of the attractive investments in recent years has been in the area of waste management. It is predicted that in coming years waste management will be among the genuine growth opportunities. Waste management does not represent high-tech revolution. It represents new needs and business opportunities that will be met with relatively simple technologies and an emphasis on efficiency and service. This example is important because we have become so engrossed in the importance of new technologies that we are in danger of assuming that technology necessarily is equated with good business. It is not. Many good businesses will remain low tech, and their cultures will reflect this reality. On the other hand, there are numerous businesses that have emphasized traditional products, manufacturing, and service, and they will have to convert to new technologies to survive. All businesses that deal in information are forced to convert from the world of paper and spoken communications to the world of electronic information. From news services to stock brokerages and educational services, the rush to new efficiencies is on through electronic and computerized media. In order to make this transition, the human culture of these organizations will need to change dramatically. Managing this change may prove to be the key play in achieving market victory.

—Does the product sold today or the product sold tomorrow contain technologies that did not exist a few years ago?

—Are the company's products manufactured, or will they soon be manufactured, utilizing new technologies in the manufacturing process?

—Are the technologies used by dominant suppliers, customers, or competitors undergoing rapid change?

The factors listed above are not intended to be an exhaustive list of cultural traits within any organization. They should, however, serve to assist planning teams in considering some of the more prominent factors that contribute to their human environment. Planning teams may identify additional factors that are of greater concern than those listed. The planning teams should define how things are today, the current culture, and they should define their idealized culture, how they would like it to be in the future. The future culture cannot be planned without understanding the forces acting upon it from without and from within. If the culture is to change, some of these influences will have to change. If the external influences are changing, the culture may have to change whether the inhabitants like it or not.

ELEVEN

Strategy: Defining Forces of Influence

Competitive success will belong to those who correctly identify those forces in the future environment, both internal and external, which determine their culture and either respond to or exert their will upon those forces.

The primary influences on the culture can be divided into influences from within—"who we are and how we are organized"; and influences from without, the "external environment." The first set of forces is controllable. To a good measure the firm can change "who we are and how we are organized," although there are limits to this control. The firm cannot suddenly change its employee population. It can plan to encourage new competencies and people with varied backgrounds and perspectives. The external environment is far less controllable, and it is that environment that is the primary consideration in the development of the strategic plan. These forces also influence the human environment. If management recognized the trends in these forces, it can plan its culture to meet the new contingencies.

Planning teams should identify all the forces that have shaped the current environment, and they should consider which of those forces are changing and will therefore require a change in the culture of the firm. The external forces include factors such as the economics of markets, changes in technology, and changes in regulation. The businesses which properly anticipate changes in these forces have a competitive advantage because they are able to plan changes in their internal environment, the types of people they employ, and the way they are organized, and change their human culture to promote the behavior that will result in successful competition.

WHO WE ARE AND HOW WE ARE ORGANIZED

People are the culture. Different sorts of people create different sorts of cultures. The culture of a meat-packing plant in Iowa will never resemble that of a New York publishing firm, nor should it. They may both exhibit the eight general cultural traits described in Part I of this book; however, their execution will look entirely different. They employ totally different people who do different things and have different priorities. Their cultures must reward different behavior and encourage different types of human development. The following are some of the "who we are and how we are organized" considerations that have determined today's culture and must be considered in the planning of tomorrow's.

1. Stereotypes: Engineers, Salespersons, and Bean Counters

While no stereotypes of professional groups are sure guides to anyone's behavior, they are also not all wrong. It is true that someone who has been trained in and worked at selling for many years develops a repertoire of behavior consistent with the selling process. Accountants do not learn the same behavior. They learn behavior that is adaptive and leads to success in their profession. This is necessary and beneficial. It only becomes problematic when a firm is dominated by people with behavior that is adaptive for one set of tasks and must suddenly demonstrate uncharacteristic performance. The "Big Eight" accounting firms have now entered an age of competition in which the CPAs are being asked to market aggressively. This is new behavior and is not simple to initiate. It contradicts the personality, training, and even values of many of the best professionals. An engineering center of a major manufacturer nowadays is asked to function as a "performance center," selling its services and responding to the desires of the manufacturing segments of the organization. The engineers have received twenty years of day-to-day conditioning that have taught them to dictate specifications to the manufacturing organization and to respond based on their own priorities. Their habits are typical of many internal staff technicians, and now they are asked to engage in selling behavior.

Many professional groups are being confronted with their stereotypical behavior and challenged to expand their skills, views, and priorities. The traditional organization has accepted and even promoted the traditional habits. The problem begins when the new organization demands a greater variety of skills. The following questions should be considered by planning teams in their identification of their current culture and in their definition of their idealized future culture:

—What behaviors are characteristic of the professionals in the organizations that promote their success?

—What behaviors are characteristic of the professionals in the organizations that inhibit their performance?

—Which behaviors characteristic of the group need to be changed or replaced to facilitate the future success of the business plan?

—Which skills need to be developed better to meet today's mission?

—Which skills need to be developed or found (i.e., new people) to meet the needs of tomorrow's mission?

2. Age/Sex

The mere mention of age and sex as factors in the management of a business will cause many a manager to reach for his or her attorney's phone number. The truth is, unfortunately, that the culture of an organization is affected by the age and sex composition of managers and employees, and a failure to consider these influences is bad business.

I recently spent time with a firm which specializes in information-systems development for mini- and microcomputers. The average age of all managers in the organization was thirty-two years. A day prior to that I had been visiting a firm with managers whose average age must have been about fifty. This firm, now attempting to diversify and change its management style, has virtually no managers in their later thirties or early forties. There is a wide age gap between the great majority of older persons and the smaller number of very young people who have been hired in the last few years. The average young age of the information-system managers has advantages and some distinct dangers. They are bright and energetic, but clearly are weak in the mature judgment that is often critical to the decision-making process. In a few years the manufacturing firm will be faced with large numbers of retirements, leaving many gaps in technical abilities, and it is hindered by a lack of the energy that is created by people in the prime of their career competing to get ahead.

There are many·organizations in our country in which there are still very few women, particularly in positions of power and influence. This is a decided cultural disadvantage for these firms, not because of EEO requirements or because women are "just as good as men." It is a disadvantage because women bring a diversity of views, perceptions, and style that enriches the consensus that determines a firm's future. The buying power of women is no secret to any marketer. Yet many companies that cater to the women's market lack the internal influences that would help them address that market. Most organizations are attempting to change their style and culture to be more facilitative and caring. These organizations are run and dominated by men who have been raised and conditioned in the macho tradition. It is a lot easier to alter that conditioning when there are alternative styles among those with whom they are interacting on a daily basis.

—What are the dominant age-sex characteristics of the organization?
—How do these characteristics influence decision making?
—How do these characteristics influence the organization's ability to respond to customers?
—How will these characteristics change in the coming years, and how will these changes affect organizational performance?
—Given the future business and external environment of the organization, what changes would be desirable in the age-sex characteristics of the group?

3. High Risk/Low Risk

We all have an orientation toward risk. This is a function of our conditioning, our investment in the status quo, and our perception of the need to change to achieve comfort in the future. A major real estate investment firm that has grown by multiples in the past few years is trying to stabilize its management and create the practices and disciplines that will ensure its success as a mature business. All the key managers of the firm were original investors, have gambled big, won, and become multimillionaires. They are high rollers who have won their independence. They are big risk takers. Not surprisingly, these executives are not good at adhering to the disciplines of reporting, following the chain of command, coaching their subordinates, or doing many of the nitty-gritty things that good managers are supposed to do. If their subordinates model their behavior, which is likely, the firm may face a demise as rapid as its ascent.

Knowing that it is very high on the risk-taking continuum, and knowing that it needs to create a cadre of managers who are a bit more conservative and more likely to manage the business, the company must develop a deliberate plan to attract and reward such managers. Such a cultural transition will not happen naturally in this firm and in many others. For each subunit of the organization management must determine what kind of risk taking is desired by the managers and employees of that unit, what are the systems and habits that are reinforcing risk taking or hindering it, and how that may change in the future. Appropriate risk taking is highly variable from one function in the organization to another. Consider the following questions for each unit of the organization:

—Do members of the organization have a tendency to be high-risk oriented or low-risk oriented?

—What types of decisions or situations require risk taking, and are people willing to take necessary risks or prone to taking excessive risks?

—Will the future business plan call for greater risk taking or less?

4. Education/Skills

The educational and skill composition of an organization affects its culture and performance. The percentage of employees who can be called "knowledge workers" is increasing, and it will continue to increase at a dramatic rate. In the future the success of most firms will depend on the ability of their employees to think and process information effectively. Genuinely "smart" companies will succeed. The business plan must match the ability of the employees to perform the knowledge functions demanded by the plan. Today it is common for a corporation to make strategic business decisions that assume a human competence and a knowledge that do not exist in the firm.

—What knowledge competencies are most prevalent within the firm today?

—What knowledge competencies will be most needed to achieve the success of the future business plan?

—What competencies can be enhanced through internal education and development, and what skills will need to be developed by recruiting new personnel?

5. Centralized/Decentralized Organization

The structure of the organization affects human behavior. People working in small decentralized units can be expected to behave in ways that will vary from those in a large centralized organization. Entrepreneurial behavior, risk taking, feelings of ownership, and personal involvement, while not assured, are more likely to be present in the decentralized organization. The centralized organization is most apt to produce more consistent behavior, tighter control, and more diverse role models.

—What type of behavior is most needed by the organization today and in the future: entrepreneurial and risk-taking behavior or disciplined and low-risk "grinding it out"?

—How does the current organization promote or hinder these behaviors?

—What inefficiencies and costs are now produced by lack of control and duplication?

—What opportunities are being lost by the lack of risk taking?

—How should the organization be restructured to meet the definition of the desired culture?

6. Many Layers/Few Layers

An organization may vary in the number of layers, whether centralized or decentralized. The Japanese automobile manufacturer, even though it is highly centralized, has few layers. By some counts, Japanese manufacturers have as few as one half the layers that some competing U.S. manufacturers have. There are obvious efficiencies in an organizational structure with few layers. There is a cost in the reduction of promotion possibilities, a highly regarded reward for the American employee. There is a growing consensus among American firms that there is a need to reduce the number of layers from top to bottom. This reduction will impact behavior in the company. Rewards for competence and achievement will have to be distributed on an organizational level rather than by promoting upward. Organizations with few layers can move more quickly, and there are likely to be fewer approval levels and less time spent convincing and impressing each successive level of management. In order to reduce the management layers, managers will have to learn to push responsibility downward, increase self-management at the bottom, and assume greater decision-making responsibility.

—How many organizational layers are there from CEO to hourly employee, and how does this number compare to competitive firms?

—Imagine the total elimination of each layer in turn, and what the consequences would be in terms of behavior of the layer below. If the consequences would not be disastrous, would the elimination of that layer be justified?

—Have employees at the bottom been trained, provided the tools, and encouraged to manage themselves to the maximum degree possible?

7. Cost Center/Profit Center

The method of keeping score on the performance of a business unit has a dramatic effect on the behavior within. Those organizations that are driven by profit and revenue capture tend to be more responsive to the needs of their clients and to be more flexible in their method of operation. Business units that are measured on cost usually operate on a longer time interval and are willing to invest in activities which may not produce a benefit for many years. Internal staff organizations are generally cost centers. Decentralized manufacturing operations or sales-marketing organizations may be profit centers. A number of large centralized firms are reorganizeing to create profit or "performance centers." These centers must sell their products or services (either internally or externally), manage their own costs and revenues, and may retain a percentage of their profits for investment within their own centers. Each type of organization requires different sets of behaviors and faces a different set of risks and rewards.

—Do managers of the business unit act to create revenues as well as costs?

—Are managers and employees rewarded for profit (or other factor of revenues to costs)?

—Are managers willing to incur the risks of long-range activities or are they hindered by focusing on short-term accounting?

The seven factors of the internal environment—who we are and how we are organized—are among the most powerful of the forces acting on the behavior of employees within the firm. In their planning efforts, managers should analyze their own organization along these dimensions, specifying how they see themselves today and how they would like to see themselves tomorrow. They can specify who they would like to be and how they would like to be organized only if they understand the definition of their current culture and the idealized culture, and if they understand the external factors that will determine their business plan. A successful plan for the culture is the product of understanding the dynamic interaction between these forces.

THE EXTERNAL ENVIRONMENT

There are a multitude of forces in the environment outside the firm that impact the behavior of those working within. The external environment of the past has shaped the culture of today; tomorrow's environment will shape the culture of the future. The corporations that will be most successful will be those with the wit to anticipate the changes in the environment to which they must respond. The culture of the firm can be managed in anticipation of those changes.

For the past several years I have been working with an enlightened chief executive officer of a power and light company in an effort to create a more market-centered, competitive culture in anticipation of future external forces that will more resemble those faced by traditional market-driven organizations. This CEO is responding to changes that he anticipates in the future rather than waiting for those changes in the external environment (in this case, deregulation and technology changes) to create a competitive disadvantage for his firm. The power company is striving to create an internal environment and culture that are consistent with open-market competition even though it does not yet exist. Successfully anticipating this change will result in a competitive advantage when it actually occurs.

For many years strategic planners have been tracking the trends and forces in the external environment and providing that input in the development of the strategic business plan. Rarely has this resulted in an effort to translate that analysis of the external environment and resulting business plan into one for the development of the internal culture. It is precisely for this reason that many strategic plans do not result in competitive success.

The following ten external forces are among those that will have the most significant impact on the human culture. The questions for consideration are geared toward understanding how the firm might respond to its analysis of the direction that these forces will take in the future.

1. Products, Services, and Customers

The nature of the products or services produced and sold by a firm has a dramatic effect on the behavior of the employees. A medical-products company that designs and produces infant respiratory monitors must have a view of quality control that is entirely different from an apparel manufacturer that can sell its second-quality goods at a reduced price. The firms which specialize in financial-planning services for large and sophisticated investors behave in ways vastly different from the financial planners whose offices can be found in large retail stores. While they may say that they are in the same business, the nature of their customers and the specifics of the services they sell dictate different talents, skills, and priorities.

—What are the characteristics of the firm's products or services that impact the talents, views, and priorities of the firm's employees.

—How will these products differ in the coming years, and how will these differences affect employee behavior?

—What are the characteristics of the customers and markets that impact employee behavior?

—How will the characteristics of the customers and markets differ in the coming years and how will those changes affect employee behavior, and will they require new employee skills and priorities?

2. Market Change/Market Stability

The degree of change in a market produces a dramatic impact on the internal functioning of a firm. Information technology companies have experienced enormously rapid changes in market preferences and competition. Texas Instruments' success in the home-computer market quickly turned to gloom when Coleco announced its Adam home-computer system. It would not be surprising if another company announced a breakthrough product within a six-month period that alters the home-computer market again with equal drama. In such an environment a "fast-moving, fast-deciding" style is essential, and the game is likely to be played by high-risk players. Low-risk players will avoid such markets.

Rapid change also has implications for manufacturing, technical development, and so forth. Rapid change produces stress, long work days, and sacrifices of personal life-style. Often one can choose the style of the business one wishes to be in. However, in recent times, changes in the marketplace have occurred that have upset the chosen life-style of many. People who entered the insurance business ten and twenty years ago could look forward to a relatively stable market and products, to customer loyalty, and to predictable income. All that has changed with the integration of financial services, and many are being forced to change contrary to their preferences.

—Are the markets and customers of the firm stable or undergoing rapid change?

—Are the managers and employees of the firm adapting to the changes doing so quickly enough?

—Will the rate of change increase or decrease in the coming years, and is management anticipating the changes and planning their response to the changes?

3. Product/Market Life Cycle

A fast-food chain specializing in health foods increases its volume and labor force by 100 percent four years in a row. A manufacturer providing sheet metal parts to the auto industry reduces its manpower by 50 percent over a two-year period. Both of these firms have distinct characteristics as functions of their maturity and growth. Because of the increased market for fast foods and health foods, the first company has hired hundreds of young, healthy-looking folks who match their customers' priorities. Because of the youth and inexperience of its employees, the company is hard pressed to meet its needs for managerial competence and judgment at every level. The sheet metal firm could not be more different. Not only are the ages and types of people different, there is a different psychology among the workers. The young employees of the health-food chain talk proudly about their healthy foods. They believe they are doing something that is superior and beneficial and has a bright future. The first concerns among the sheet metal workers are job security, number of years to retirement, and prayers for the survival of their company. Rapid growth or decline present totally different strategies for managing the human environment. Each presents problems, challenges, and advantages.

—What has been the rate of growth of the business and how has that impacted the behavior of employees?

—What will be the likely growth pattern in the next few years?

—How will that growth or decline affect the human environment and what steps can management take to anticipate the problems associated with those changes?

4. Technology Change/Technology Stability

A producer of industrial control systems is a leader in its field. It has a stable base of customers and a reputation for reliability and service. Comfortable in its business, it ignored the development of digital technology. Suddenly its competitors release lines of digital control systems which compete directly with its analog systems. Its design and development department lacks the skills to pursue digital controls. Having worked with analog systems for years, the engineers have great faith in them and do not believe that customers will switch as a result of the new technology. The culture of this systems company was based on technological stability. It was not sensitive to change, and when change emerged it wished to ignore it. If a company is to be responsive to changes in technology, it must have a cadre of the right people in the right positions. These people must be rewarded for innovation, keeping their own skills at the leading edge of technology change, and managers must be willing to listen and consider future possibilities.

—Has the past rate of technology change been rapid or stable?

—How has this past rate conditioned attitudes and behavior within the firm?

—During the next two to five years, what is the anticipated rate of technology change?

—What changes in people and organizations will be required to meet the coming changes?

5. Regulation: Tight Control/Loose Control

In recent years there has been a monumental shift in regulation toward loose control, so-called deregulation. The airline industry, financial services, communications, and interstate trucking have all witnessed transformations in regulatory control with fundamental implications for the management of their businesses. Tight regulation increases business stability, reduces competition, and reduces price-cost sensitivity, innovation, and the rate of customer response.

Deregulation reverses all of these. American Telephone & Telegraph did anticipate deregulation of the telephone business and began taking steps to become more market driven and responsive long before deregulation actually occurred. The measures that they took represented a mammoth cultural transformation—from a true monopoly to a sales-driven competitor. Deregulation is likely to continue in coming years, increasing competitive pressures. The need to change the behavior of employees to being customer-responsive and competitive is a major challenge of literally hundreds of corporations.

—What is the current impact of regulation on the behavior of employees within the firm?

—Will regulation increase or decrease in coming years?

—What changes in behavior should occur to respond to changes in operations and competition resulting from regulatory changes?

6. Resource Availability

Predicting resource availability has been a major challenge for planners in recent years. The dramatic shifts in petroleum supply in recent years have produced billion-dollar nightmares for corporate planners. Electric utilities have switched from oil to coal and back to oil with the changes in fuel cost. The availability of human resources has also produced shifts in corporate behavior. In the case of engineers, particularly electrical engineers, the movement has been from undersupply to oversupply and back to undersupply in five-year cycles. For large, technology-oriented firms, these shifts in human-resource availability represent significant considerations in their planning. Changes in resource availability change the behavior of everyone associated with the utilization of those resources. When petroleum was scarce, corporate buyers had one set of priorities that changed dramatically. Energy conservation programs, goals, and rewards for reduced use were common several years ago. Today they are far less prominent. When human competence is scarce, the price of that competence goes up and the demands that skilled individuals will make on the organization will increase.

—What are the major categories of resources upon which the organization depends?

—What shifts can be expected in those resources in coming years and how will those shifts impact behavior within the firm?

—What actions can the firm take to respond to these changes?

*   *   *

The six factors listed above are only a few among the many forces in the external environment that may have shaped the current culture and which may change to alter that culture. Other forces may include economic factors (inflation, tax policies, interest rates, and growth in GNP) and political factors (local, national, and international). Planning teams should discuss all of them and focus on those which may significantly affect their business in the years to come. If these changes can be anticipated, the culture of the firm may be managed by altering how the company is managed and "who we are and how we are organized."

The planning process should be interactive and ongoing. A plan for the culture of the firm is not something that is done once and then put to bed. It should be designed as an involvement procedure, utilizing managers and employees at every level in self-examination, imagining an ideal future, and working on plans to attain that future. The review and modification of these plans should be done at least annually. The planning teams should bear responsibility not only for the construction of the plan, but for monitoring its progress.

TWELVE

Tactics: Getting Change Started

> I know of no corporation which has succeeded in achieving a significant change in its culture without the strong and active leadership of a senior and powerful executive.

Strategy must be translated into tactics. Creating a shared vision of the future is the first tactic. Involving all the managers of the organization in planning the idealized corporate culture will initiate the change process. In order to achieve the realization of the new culture, it will be necessary to marshal all available forces. Changing the culture requires examples, training, direction, coaching, reinforcement, and systems which support the new behavior.

The culture of an organization is the sum of the habits of its members. Habits are the result of years of observation, trials, and rewards. They are well learned. As anyone who has attempted to change habits knows, they die hard. Dieting, quitting smoking, or reducing one's drinking are all tough challenges, and changing management habits is no less a challenge.

Most efforts to change management style fail. They fail because they do not face up to the difficulties involved in changing habits. They typically create a change in "intentional behavior," that which is under the control of a deliberate, and usually short-lived, program. The worst case is the senior executive who decides that participation is in. He lets his subordinates know that he thinks participation is keen, and they find themselves agreeing with true conviction. They go forth, arrange training, and pass on the edict. There are some initial efforts, usually in the form of holding more meetings, the character of which most closely resembles the old staff meetings. A few months later someone recognizes that they are spending too much time in unproductive meetings and the effort is no longer made. Intentional behavior occurred for about as long as might be expected, and habitual behavior soon assumed its dominant role.

The eight primary values proposed in this book all represent a complex of habits. They will not be achieved without the noble struggle that accompanies any alteration in long-held customs. Consensus, for example, will not be achieved by one training program, direction, plea, or other form of intervention. It will be accomplished only as a result of gradual, consistent, and determined effort spanning a number of years.

Consensus, empiricism, or other cultural characteristics represent a milieu of habitual responses. These responses are of four types: overt behavior, mental habits, emotions, and values. Overt behaviors are those responses that can be observed and counted. They are the meetings held, the tones of voice and the movements of the eye. Mental habits are just as significant manifestations of a culture as overt behavior, yet far less apparent. People of different cultures think in different patterns. The Japanese, Russians, and Chinese all think differently. These thought patterns are the result of long cultural training and have at least as much impact on how managers manage and workers work as does overt behavior. Peoples of different cultures also have different emotional response patterns. The Latin temperament or the Scandinavian detachment are genuine cultural differences. Values differ as well: the importance of family, clan, corporation, the interpretation of ethical behavior, and the willingness to sacrifice self-interest, all represent the conditioning of our culture. It is the composite of all four types of response and their interaction that determine whether consensus is a characteristic of the normative culture of the organization. All these habits must be altered if the corporation is to achieve the establishment of a new culture.

LEADERSHIP AND CHANGE

Change requires leadership. It is in the normal course of events for patterns of behavior to continue as they have been. Behavior and cultures resist change and are likely to shift significantly only when stimulated by strong leadership. Executives are often confused about where this leadership should come from. Isn't the training department responsible for developing management skills? Doesn't the human resources V.P. have someone on his staff who takes care of organization development? The fact is, these people are technicians who completely lack the power required to create change. I know of no corporation which has succeeded in achieving a significant change without the strong and active leadership of a powerful senior executive.

It is most difficult to provide strong leadership of change and at the same time serve as an example of consensus management. Every executive with whom I am familiar who has provided the leadership for change has been accused of commanding that change. So be it. While it is best to create the change while practicing involvement, it is a lesser sin to err in the direction of command than to fail to create the changes that are vital to the success of the business.

When Samuel H. Turner became president of Life of Virginia, an insurance company, he was convinced that change was an urgent priority. Life of Virginia was not in trouble. It had been in business successfully for 112 years, had a strong base of recognition in the South, 1,100 agents, the traditional products, and loyal customers. The culture of the company was what might be called "peaceful." If Sam Turner had thought that the external environment would remain peaceful, he would have been content to work gradually to achieve incremental improvements in the business. But his analysis convinced him that a revolution was imminent in the life insurance industry in the form of new, nontraditional products and new competitors. Life of Virginia could either be a victim of these changes or take advantage of them. He chose the latter course.

If the majority of the senior managers had initially shared Turner's views, the change process would have been easier. They didn't. Turner readily admits that he dictated change. He began with the introduction of what was then the revolutionary "universal life" policy; he created new distribution channels; he sponsored new advertising that challenged the industry; and he initiated the development of new internal systems that would eventually reduce turnaround time on key service functions from several weeks to forty-eight hours. He created an enthusiasm for the new directions by speaking constantly to employee groups. He repeatedly used key words and phrases like "sense of urgency," "commitment," and "being first." He focused on sources of energy by walking around work areas before, during, and after normal work hours to identify and recognize employees who were performing above and beyond the call of duty. The excitement of change began to produce heroes and heroines. One woman, who was on a task force working on the development of new systems, was hospitalized at the height of the task force's work. She checked herself out of the hospital, without her doctor's approval, and drove straight to her office in the middle of the night to resume her work so that the task force could meet its deadline. Each time Turner spoke, he told this and other stories about employees who were making the change possible.

During a three-year period, Life of Virginia made a quantum leap. The company assumed a leadership position in industry, it developed a nationwide distribution network, and during the first six months of 1983, individual life product sales increased 100 percent over those of 1982. Now that momentum has been gained and the revolution has quieted down, Sam Turner is working to increase participation and involvement at every level. However, his assessment that command leadership was necessary to initiate rapid change was undoubtedly correct.

The style of change, command to consensus, properly reflects just how threatening the external environment is. If the external threat is not real, the executive would be well advised to create the change through greater involvement and the development of a shared vision with his team of senior managers. However, when the executive firmly believes that rapid change is necessary to the well-being of the enterprise, he has a responsibility to act to create that change even though his command style will not be appreciated by all of those who are below him.

TALKING IT UP

A number of years ago Jim Renier became president of Honeywell Control Systems. He knew the organization well from his many years with the company. With a Ph.D. in physics, enormous energy, and a sincere dedication to improving the human condition, Renier had developed his own vision of the responsibilities of the organization to its members, and he articulated his philosophy in terms of developing self-esteem. Renier spoke to every management group within Honeywell, and shared his vision of the corporation's responsibility, the value of the individual, and the manager's responsibility to promote self-esteem among the organization's members. Not everyone shared his passion for this subject, and there were those who considered it a phase that he surely would pass through and which they could wait out. However, the phase persisted, and it was followed by numerous actions to put his ideas into practice. Gradually managers began to take his ideas seriously and to act in ways which they felt were consistent with his philosophies.

Talk about the philosophy of self-esteem became common throughout the organization. Each manager felt a need to express his own variation of this philosophy. It was a sign of being on the team. Change had begun.

Employees also began to listen and talk about the philosophy. As they began to think about these ideas, they began to question company policies and practices. They even confronted Renier directly with questions about minority and handicapped hiring and treatment, questions that were not pleasant to deal with. However, opening the mind to new ideas usually produces conflict. Change produces conflict. Old cultures, ideas and practices, habits never shift without irritation. The organization in which there is no irritation or conflict is one that is not changing or growing. It is in trouble. The healthy organization, the one which is undergoing constructive change, witnesses conflict and questioning, but is able to struggle in an honest and open way with those questions. It is this process that Renier's "talking it up" at Honeywell initiated.

Our culture and values, our way of behaving in the organization, are a function of ideas. Ideas are expressed through talking, and sometimes in writing. Executives do not do a lot of writing, so what they say is taken as the substance of their ideas and values. Subordinates listen very closely. Just how closely would frighten most executives. Employees often do not hear what executives would like them to hear. However, they usually hear what really does matter. The true values and priorities make it through the flak. The alleged priorities of today often go unheard. Employees are sensitive to those priorities that will result in meaningful consequences. Directions or priorities that will produce no results for the individual generally produce no change in his or her behavior. The employee knows that those ideas or practices shall pass and life will have changed little. However, when substantive messages are repeated and reinforced often by the significant person in the organization, employees and managers do respond. They react particularly if the message expresses their own values and elevates their image of the organization.

The chief executive officer and senior executives are the residents in the chair of leadership. They must articulate the desired values of the organization. A key ingredient in any significant corporate change effort is the promotion and marketing of the new values to the organization by the senior managers. If this is not done, the effort is likely to be perceived as one more in a long string of superficial efforts to improve performance, none of which has had a lasting effect on the organization.

PLANNING

When an executive or a management team decides that a change in culture is desirable, the planning process begins. Initially this may be done informally. The executive may begin to research efforts in other corporations, determine who in his own company has relevant expertise or experience, and he may begin to contact consultants who assist in this type of change. Often the executive will designate a subordinate to carry the ball and plan the effort. The process of organizational change is so clumsy and unscientific that the poor designee often suffers considerable strain.

It is at this point that consultants can be helpful. An intelligent, experienced, and well-organized consultant can help bring stability to culture change. Planning necessitates a model to determine where the organization is currently and where it can or should go, based on various considerations impacting its current and future business. Consultants are famous for their matrices, three-dimensional squares, circles, and so forth, all visualizing a pet model that lays out in incredible order the "five elements of truth" according to their view of life in the organization. Of course, these models no more represent the true world than any jumble of words. However, they do serve an entirely useful and legitimate purpose. One of the legitimate functions of a consultant is to help bring order to the thinking of the client. It is the client who best knows the conditions within his organization. The consultant, with his model in hand (or in mind), can help the client organize his thinking about the current situation. Organized thinking leads to action. Disorganized thinking leads to confusion and anxiety. Consultants may help simply by using models to sort the existing information and to demonstrate to their clients that they actually know more about their own situation than they thought previously.

Planning usually should begin with an assessment of the current situation. Some consulting firms will conduct elaborate and expensive evaluations of the client's current state. These evaluations are often a poor investment. The best assessments are conducted in a manner that involves the client's managers in the process. Assessments done entirely by the consulting firm may produce findings that are not biased by the views of the client's managers. However, they will be biased by the consultant's views. There is no avoiding biases in an assessment procedure. The criteria against which any organization is judged are biases. Better to involve the firm's managers so that they understand the judgments and believe that they were reached fairly. The skilled consultant can lead a group of managers through a self-assessment process so that they believe the results of the evaluation are their own judgments about themselves. They agree on their own priorities and evaluations. The managers of the target organization generally feel good about this process because they know that the consultant has demonstrated respect for their judgments, has not imposed his own views, and has helped them organize their thinking. This leads to commitment, trust, mutual respect, and a shared vision of where the managers would like to go and how to get there together.

Many organizations first entering into culture change take entirely too long to get the process moving toward some form of constructive action. This delay often results in a loss of enthusiasm or priority among the executives who initiated the process. Planning should require no more than three or four months. Delay is often caused by the executive's desire to achieve complete consensus or buy-in by all his managers. This is futile, since change will not be achieved if the principles of volunteering or complete consensus are adhered to. The executive should make a reasonable effort to involve his team of senior managers in the decision to change, to agree on the general direction or nature of that change, and to review the action plan. However, he cannot abandon his individual responsibility for achieving the strategic goals of the corporation. The CEO is responsible for seeing that change does occur within a reasonable period of time.

TRAINING

Managers have entirely too much faith in training. Corporations spend huge sums each year to train managers to behave well. Most of this money is wasted. Typically the manager will be singled out to go to the corporate training center or a training program put on by an outside agency for three days to learn Management by Objectives, Listening Skills, or Conducting Performance Appraisals. The course may be addressed to the specific skill he needs most. It may be well presented. The instructor may be brilliant and witty, the student attentive and enthralled. The student has what some trainers like to call an "ah-ha experience." This is when the student says to himself, "Of course, this all makes sense! What an idiot I have been all these years! If only I had had this course . . ." He swears that this has changed his life and he is a new person. The trainer loves it. The best trainers have learned to maintain their sanity by programming such responses and sharing the joy of the student (trainers are privy to few other satisfactions).

Alas, ecstasy does not last long. The newly trained manager returns to the real world of his office to find a stack of problems on his desk, his boss in a huff over the latest crisis, complaints from customers, suppliers, or subordinates, and whatever other distractions consume his normal day. Being the good trouper that he is, he dives in to attack the mess. It is weeks or perhaps months later that our hero spots the three-ring loose-leaf binder, his only visible symbol of his fond memories of salvation. A regretful sigh and an "Oh, yes. I'll have to get to that soon" are likely the last gasps produced by the three days of management training.

It is a somewhat well-preserved secret among trainers that students remember about 15 to 20 percent of what they hear during the course of a training session. They then proceed to act on 15 to 20 percent of what they remember of that. Training conducted in the traditional fashion is quite unproductive in creating actual change in the way things are really done. The culture of the organization, the habits of its members are no more likely to change in this manner than a smoker is likely to quit after seeing a film on the evils of smoking.

Training is, however, a necessary ingredient of the change process. Managing in new ways requires the development of new skills.

This is the function of training. However, training should never be viewed as the end. It is only a preceding step that may help achieve the end. The following steps will help to improve training's productivity:

1. Training should follow the specification of precisely which behaviors are to follow. What will managers do following the training? Do they know they will have to do certain things? If not, why not? If managers enter the training situation with clear expectations that they must return to the real world and initiate team problem solving, set objectives, or conduct performance appraisals in a certain way, their attitude toward training will be entirely different than if they lack these expectations. How training will be conducted will also vary. Training that leads to action should be experiential, should include criterion testing, and should incorporate planning the application of such action to the work setting. The trainer should be held accountable for the successful implementation back on the farm, not for good reviews in the session.

2. Managers should be trained as a team. All the managers in a plant, office, or region should be trained together. Group psychology generally works against the adoption of the lessons learned in training. When managers are sent to training as individuals and are asked to return and apply their new skills, they are generally asked to contradict the norms of the group. They are required to be "cultural deviants." Psychologically this is unsafe. With the entire group being trained together the force of group psychology can be used to support the new behavior. The managers can all be asked to commit—to their peers, to engage in the new activity. If they are all engaged in change together, then failure to change can become the deviance that is difficult to adhere to. It is important that managers all have the same language and degree of understanding. I recommend that two levels of managers be trained together, and in some cases three levels. This is an opportunity to communicate to the subordinate manager that this activity is important. It is common to hear people say, "If he's gonna do it, so am I."

3. Training should incorporate cases and experiences from the work setting of those being trained. This is possible when large

numbers of managers are involved and in groups from the same organization. The relevance of training is one of the most common complaints of managers. It is the responsibility of the trainer to get in touch with the real world of the manager and make the material relevant.

4. Training should be spread out over time. Unfortunately, we all have our limits as to the amount of material we can digest at any one sitting. While we are on the subject, how long can a manager sit in one place without going bananas? My experience says three days. If a manager is comfortable sitting for more than three days, he is probably a clerk disguised as a manager. Any trainer who cannot present an overdose of material in three days is probably stretching his subject matter out in a manner that will produce boredom, if not an overdose. Shorter doses such as two-hour sessions, once a week for a number of months, are preferable to three-day sessions. Obviously the amount of material and the number of training sessions are functions of the objectives.

5. Training should initiate action. What action is the manager to take after the workshop is complete? The trainer should design an "Action Planning" process within each training session. Each manager should select some performance that he or she would like to change, apply the lessons learned in the training to the improvement of that performance, and design the specific steps to be taken in the workshop. If the individual gets out the door without making a formal commitment to specific action, the action is unlikely to happen. Weight Watchers and Alcoholics Anonymous have both been successful in producing change in some of the most resilient habits precisely because of the psychology of group support, public commitment, and peer approval. Surely management training can incorporate the same principles to change behaviors that are almost as resistant to change.

THIRTEEN

Tactics: Making It Stick

> It is behavior that results in reinforcement that becomes habitual, a part of the normal culture, and the ability to provide reinforcement will become the most critical management skill.

If the culture is to change, managers must behave in new ways. They may learn about new behavior in training, but only as they practice the behavior and experience reinforcement will new habits take hold. Creating this practice and reinforcement is what will make them stick.[1]

CREATING ACTION

The corporation invests in training to cause managers to behave in new ways and to achieve improved performance from their employees. Any manager who participates in training should be expected to do something differently.

Precisely what action is desired should be planned prior to the training.[2] However, I have utilized a common sequence of actions that has worked well in the implementation of productivity improvement and culture-change efforts.

Training is conducted in weekly two-hour sessions over a four- to six-month period. Following each session the managers implement what they have learned. "Action Plans" are selected and designed by each manager during the first two or three months. These Action Plans incorporate the lessons learned during training. The manager is free to select one measurable and specific performance variable that he or she is concerned about improving. Then the manager decides how he is going to measure the performance, graph the baseline data, determine what actions to take to influence the performance, and design an evaluation plan.[3] These plans are openly discussed in the workshops, and each manager's description of the plan becomes a public commitment, witnessed by his peer group. These Action Plans usually involve a new analysis of the human behavior that contributes to the performance problem, a plan to involve employees in the solution, data-based feedback, and positive reinforcement to the employees for improved performance. However, the plans are essentially individual responsibilities. They do not represent any radical shift in the nature of management or individual roles.

During the fourth and fifth months, the weekly sessions focus on the skills of leading team meetings, personal listening skills, and problem solving. During this time a team management system is set up. This system generally involves every person within the organization. Every manager is designated the team leader of those employees who report to him. Every manager is also on his superior's team. This results in a sequence of interlocking teams from the top of the organization down to and including the hourly employee. The system is never voluntary. It is an organizational commitment to a new way of managing. A schedule of team meetings is agreed to by all the managers. Team meetings usually occur once a week and there is a general planned agenda. The agenda will usually include the following:

a. A review of the team's performance for the prior week. This will usually be done by showing graphs of the key data variables for the team. The team comes to understand these charts and graphs very well.

b. The team will set improvement objectives for next week on each of these data variables.

c. The team will problem-solve high and low performances, and brainstorm ideas to improve any performance of concern.

d. The team leader will make a point of reinforcing the behavior of an individual or of the team for any outstanding performance.

These team meetings are specific, structured activities that give every manager the opportunity to try out his or her new skills. The mere knowledge before the training that these team meetings are expected in itself significantly increases the learning that occurs in the training.

Needless to say, many managers and supervisors are not comfortable with such team meetings. However, they are provided with hands-on assistance that will help them over the most difficult first few. The first meetings are undoubtedly more for griping than for constructive performance review and goal setting. However, this is a normal transition that must be gone through. The manager is taught to respond to the gripes either with a sincere "I'll pass that along" or "I'll find out about that." The focus of energies is redirected by the manager to "What do you folks think we can do about that?"

These team meetings are a structured way for the manager and supervisor to learn how to involve his team in the management process. As this involvement effort succeeds, the employees begin to feel more ownership for the results of their work. They begin to believe in their own ability to contribute to the real work of the plant, to the thinking and decision making that determine its success. This produces ideas, enthusiasm, and more productive work. This, in turn, reinforces the manager in his attempt at a new way of managing.

During the sixth through eighth months, the sessions may focus on the implementation of Quality Control Circles, additional management skills in particular need of emphasis, or on the development of self-managed work teams. During these months, training for the hourly employee is also initiated to help them participate in self-managed teams and problem solving. All of this training is followed by specific planned action.

Training that does not result in planned action, followed with reinforcement and accountability, is simply a poor investment of management time.

COACHING

There is no magic. Change, like most worthwhile things in life, requires more work, persistence, resilience, and a touch of humility, than any other ingredients. Efforts that succeed often do so not because their designers hit on the right formula at first shot, but because the participants toughed it out.

It is my experience that even when the training is well designed and executed, even when there is excellent commitment on the part of the managers, even when they design and share action plans within the training, only half the participants will actually implement those Action Plans. About 60 or 70 percent of the plans that are implemented will produce some improvement on the first round. This degree of follow-through is too low. It will not produce the pervasive change in the way things are normally done in the organization. The cultural norms are still in control and the new way of doing things is likely to be overcome by the old.

What happens after the training does more to determine the success of the change effort than what happens before or during the training itself. This is little understood by most trainers. The trainer's problem is over at the conclusion of training. The manager's problem has just begun.

It is the coaching that follows training and is based on the agreed-upon Action Plans that does more to produce actual and lasting change than anything else. The manager who has been working in the same negative, controlling, individualistic way for twenty years, for example, will not change his style of management with ease. He needs help. Someone has to sit in on his team meetings and give him feedback on how he handled the employee who wouldn't stop talking. Someone has to ask him when he is going to recognize the individual who just set a new quality record for his job. Someone needs to help him problem-solve when the Action Plan simply does not produce the desired results. And someone has to cheer him on, tell him he is great, wonderful, deserving of all sorts of accolades, when he has put forth the considerable effort that it does require to change management style.

This is a role for the consultant, internal or external. It has been my experience that an internal and an external consultant work best together at this task: The external consultant assists in training the internal consultant, turning over all of his "learned-on-the-street" tricks for making things happen.

One of my earliest experiences implementing productivity improvement programs was in textile mills in Georgia and South Carolina. Training had been conducted for all the mill supervisors, and they were proceeding to implement their Action Plans. They were working and generating a lot of enthusiasm. In the weekly management meetings, the supervisors were asked to show their graphs on their performance improvement projects. As the supervisors went around the room, they all had an enthusiastic story of how their employees had responded favorably and how the numbers had begun to improve.

The turn of one of the last supervisors came; he was an old fellow named Matt who had probably worked in the mill for thirty years. The poor guy got up to show his graph, and it was one of the most perfectly straight lines you could imagine. Matt explained that he had set a goal with his employees; he had showed them the graph; and he had reinforced those who were doing a good job. It just wasn't working. This same procedure was working for other managers. Why not for him? Matt was near retirement, had given his life to the plant, and wanted to be part of this experience that everyone else seemed to be enjoying. His failure was visibly disturbing to him.

The consultant asked to meet with Matt the next morning. The consultant went over each step that Matt had been through. He then asked to go with him as he walked out on the weave-room floor to meet his employees, and to recognize one of his weavers who had had an exceptional performance the day before. The consultant followed behind, observing the interaction between Matt and the employees. When he came to the weaver who had performed well, Matt pulled out his graph, showed it to him, and, in a manner that was to say the least lacking enthusiasm, told him he had done a good job. The weaver responded with a puzzled look. The words "You did a good job" and the manner of the supervisor, which he knew well from years of association, simply did not fit together. Once they had returned to the privacy of the supervisor's office, the consultant coached Matt. They role-played the situation over and over again. The consultant made Matt practice smiling. He had him practice saying, "You reeeally did a greeat job last week!" It was a struggle, but in a few weeks there were reports that Matt was a different person. People wanted to know what we had done to him.

This is the nitty-gritty work of change. This is the tiring and tedious though rewarding process that makes things happen and stick. Unfortunately, too many professionals in the business of creating change are not willing to bother with this truly tough work. They would rather play the guru who bounces into town to give his inspiring message and bounces out, with no need to worry about the payoff for the bewildered supervisor who is not sure who or what has come and gone.

Perhaps the most neglected group of individuals when it comes to receiving help to change are the senior executives. The unfortunate truth is that training and development professionals are afraid of senior executives. They are, therefore, not very willing to stick their necks out and push for senior executives to participate in training or, God forbid, to give them feedback on their own management style. However, it is precisely the core of senior executives who need the most help. They need help the most not because they are the worst, but because their behavior is the most important in creating the total change desired in the organization. Their behavior patterns are among the most resilient to change because senior executives have been reinforced in them for many years. At least unconsciously they believe that their style of management has been the cause of their successes, and, therefore, there is little reason to change. Undoubtedly they have been effective or they would not have been promoted. However, their effectiveness may have been predicated upon the rules of the old culture. With the culture changing, the rules of effectiveness change, and their management styles, well ingrained, may not keep up.

One of the most rewarding consulting experiences I have had is in conducting personalized feedback to executives. This is a service that is directed at the most senior executives, and it is designed to assist them in developing their own management abilities. The senior executive is interviewed to obtain his views of his style, what he perceives to be his strengths and weaknesses as a manager. The focus is on his communication ability, decision making, expectations for subordinates, ability to provide feedback and recognition, and other keys to his effectiveness. All his subordinates, and possibly his peers are interviewed. After digesting the input, we put together our own view of his strengths and weaknesses. Then we sit down with the manager and feed back this information along with a specific plan for self-development.

What has been most gratifying about conducting this feedback has been the response of the executives. One CEO recently told me that in his twenty years as a manager and in dozens of management development experiences, this was the first time that someone actually told him, in an objective and unbiased fashion, what he really did well and what he needed to do differently. This has been a common reaction. Senior executives need to know and want to how they are doing. Unfortunately, the man or woman at the top of a corporation is the person least likely to get the honest and objective feedback that results in constructive change. Providing this type of feedback should be a top priority of management development during the next decade.

The senior executive who models the behaviors that are desired from his subordinates is one of the most important ingredients in change. Verbal support for principles and programs is nice, but behavioral support, action, produces results. Leadership is not dead, but in many organizations it has been taking a long nap. When senior managers stop carping about what their subordinates are not doing and begin setting examples, leadership will have awakened.

The coaching role performed by the consultant should be assumed by the manager. It is the job of every manager to help his subordinates succeed. The consultant should gradually begin to teach each manager how to coach his subordinates. Gradually less coaching by the outsider is needed and more is done through the management line. When an interlocking team system is functioning from top to bottom in the organization, those teams gradually take on the coaching role. Each manager presents his performance to the team, describes his Action Plan to improve that performance, and gets input from his team members. If this is functioning well, less and less coaching by outsiders is needed.

REINFORCEMENT: MAKING PERFORMANCE MATTER

New behavior becomes habitual after it has been demonstrated and repeatedly reinforced. Reinforcement is any desirable consequence following a performance that results in that performance being strengthened or maintained. The primary contribution of behavioral psychology is its empirical analysis of the relationship between stimulus-response-consequence.[4] Exhaustive research within organizations and in dozens of other environments has repeatedly demonstrated the power of consequences on performance.[5] If the culture of an organization is to change, there must be a change in the pattern of reinforcement. The old culture has been maintained by the past history of reinforcement, and the new one will have to be established with the help of a new pattern of reinforcement.

Traditional corporate cultures are characterized by a predominant use of negative consequences to control performance.[6] I met with a division general manager and two plant managers in whose plants we had been implementing an employee involvement effort. The topic turned to the need to encourage more recognition for good performance within the plants. I suggested that it was important that the plant managers make a regular practice of "catching" something their subordinates are doing well as a model for other managers within the plant. I explained that everyone in the organization tends to model themselves on those above them. This naturally led to the topic of the division manager reinforcing the plant manager. Both plant managers strongly emphasized that they didn't need to be patted on the back by their division manager. "I know when I'm doing my job. I've been working for Tom for five years and I don't expect him to be telling me when I'm doing a good job. He lets me know when I've got a problem and if he doesn't say anything to me then I know I'm all right. I don't need him patting me on the back." It is a characteristic of our macho culture that strong managers don't need a pat on the back. The need for recognition is perceived as a sign of weakness. Self-sufficiency, not having to lean on or need others, is part of the male personality that influences management style. This has led many managers to assume that they do not need to reinforce their subordinates.

The successful efforts to create a new corporate culture are those that invariably incorporate a heavy dose of recognition. The best kind of reinforcement is a sincere appreciation by manager and peers for outstanding work. This serendipitous recognition, however, cannot be relied upon. Relying on it assumes that the managers possess the desired habit of catching good performance. Unfortunately, most are more likely to ignore it. Reinforcement must be programmed within the process of change.

This programming can be accomplished in a number of ways. The consultant who is coaching managers on their efforts has the responsibility to assure that good performances are not ignored. Requirements to identify a certain number of outstanding performers each week, month, quarter, and year should be established at different levels within the organization. Awards of all sorts should be used. The awards may be money, gifts, or plaques, or they may be of value precisely because of their creative nature. For example, a manufacturing plant wanted to increase the number of suggestions for improvement submitted through an employee suggestion program.

The plant was not in very good financial condition, so a deliberate effort was made to think of rewards that would not be costly. The employees suggested selecting the best idea of the month and giving a monthly award. They suggested a T-shirt. On the front of the T-shirt they wanted the words "I HAD THE BEST IDEA—JAN-UARY, 1983." On the back of the T-shirt they wanted a large picture of the plant manager's face. The employees regarded this as extremely humorous, and they competed for the T-shirt. No one outside this organization could have predicted this would be an award the employees could get enthusiastic about. The employees are often the ones who, when asked, can devise the most inexpensive yet powerful forms of recognition.

It is also important that the most potent types of recognition the organization can dispense are used to reinforce the new culture. Promotions are particularly important. A culture-change effort will produce heroes: the individuals who stick their necks out, try new approachess to management and make them work. Those who do take this initiative are often the ones with the most leadership potential. These individuals are engaging in leadership behavior when they place themselves in the forefront of change. The entire organization will be watching to see if they are rewarded for their risk taking. They will also be watching to see if those who exhibit the characteristics that are consistent with the new culture are promoted. If promotions do not begin to reflect this selection, the change effort will not have achieved the legitimacy it otherwise would.

SUPPORTIVE ORGANIZATION AND SYSTEMS

Behavior in the organization is a function of past learning, current interpersonal influences, and the influences of the organization and systems within the corporation. If there is to be a new competitive spirit, the organization and systems must be designed to support it. Many of the existing systems and structures work directly counter to that spirit. The information system that inhibits the manager or worker from knowing his score, the compensation system that fails to differentiate between high and low performers, or the organization that makes it impossible for the individual to identify with and feel a part of a team, these must all be changed. There is not enough space here to present a thorough analysis of all the systems within a corporation. Therefore, I will merely attempt to touch on some of the key elements that are most necessary to support the new culture.

The two most significant organizational weaknesses in the American corporation are the failure to encourage teamwork and excessive layers of management. The entire organization should be structured to create team identity, team score keeping, team problem solving, and team victory. The greater use of genuine teams and the acceptance of responsibility by those teams result in the need for fewer layers of management.

A manufacturing plant in California in which every employee reported to a different supervisor virtually every week recently implemented an improvement effort. The plant operated on three shifts and a shift rotation procedure was used in which employees were rotated throughout a four-day work week while supervisors maintained a constant schedule. Therefore, a supervisor's team was made up of different combinations of workers each week. To implement and utilize a team system among the workers was extremely difficult and cumbersome. I am sure that whoever designed this system had what appeared to be a good reason, but clearly understood nothing about supervision or teamwork. It is virtually impossible to gain the benefits of helping employees track their own performance and develop team goals if they are working on different locations, within different teams, and for different supervisors each week.

This phenomenon also occurs at the management level. One major oil firm has conducted what it calls a "management development" process by rotating managers every eighteen months. The managers in this corporation acknowledge that it takes approximately twelve months for a manager to become competent. Within six months after that, the individual can expect to be rotated to another assignment. This movement usually involves moving to another part of the country. It proved very difficult to work with the management at one of its major refineries because the instability of the team prevented establishing trust, common understanding, goals, and methods of operation. It appeared that every manager in the refinery was working to clean up the mess from the previous manager by instituting some new way of managing things. Unfortunately, just as the manager got things organized, he was on his way to another assignment and his replacement set to work to clean up the mess he perceived he had inherited. This constant movement and instability in the team was a major detriment to performance, was developing managers who were "Lone Rangers," riding into town to shoot up the bad guys and ride out quickly before the dust settled and the genuine results of the effort could be perceived.

The information systems within the corporation may be divided into three types: those required for financial control, those for operational control, and those utilized for management control and decision making. It is the management information systems that are of most concern in creating the competitive culture.

A primary purpose of management information systems is to provide scores by which the manager may know whether he is succeeding or failing, improving or falling behind. Management information systems should report the key indicators of an organization's performance in a timely and understandable manner. The great weakness in most current information systems is not that they fail completely to accomplish this goal, but that they do not accomplish it for the right people. Management information systems have been designed for and by senior managers, and they have designed them with their needs in mind. They know their scores. You can be sure that in most organizations the senior managers of a division know what the key indicators of performance are for that division.

These managers can be compared to the owners of a football team. They bear some responsibility for the performance and certainly have a great deal of interest. However, it is not they who control the performance. In many organizations, the owners, head coach, and assistant coaches all know the score. Yet the players on the field, the first-line supervisors, and workers do not. The information systems have not been designed with the worker in mind and often do not provide feedback on peformance in a manner that is timely and understandable to the employee, who is the one who can actually do something about it. In many cases managers are afraid to share performance data with the worker. Some firms believe that if workers know how they are actually performing, they will relax. Everyone who is knowledgeable about the research on feedback's effect on human behavior knows that the reverse is true.

The second major flaw in the data systems is that information is presented in a terribly confusing fashion. Each manager should receive a simple report each week with the key data variables listed. What is needed is a system that consolidates the usual confusion of reports to a simple report indicating those that should be recognized for a positive accomplishment and those that should be the focus for improvement. Such a simple and clear reporting system can be implemented at every level of the organization, including the hourly team level.

Our corporations are flooded with data. A major task in the next decade will be to organize the data flow so that the individual receives information which focuses his mental energies on the right activities, provides the recognition for good performance, and helps managers know who needs their help to upgrade poor performance.

Conclusion

Much of the civilized world is now in a period of adolescence, struggling to leave the selfishness of childhood but not having attained quite the maturity to accept the unpretentious partnerships of adulthood. The consequences of conflicts have escalated to unacceptable heights. The significant decisions are best made in a manner flattering to no one's ego. And few actions on the part of leaders are met with appreciation.

The business institutions that produce the wealth of society, and upon whose shoulders rest the expectations of increasing goods and services at decreasing costs, will be the vanguard in the effort to maximize the output and integration of human energy. The privately owned business organization has been in the past and will be in the future the first to experiment, sometimes failing but inevitably succeeding in its efforts to innovate and find the means of maximizing productivity. It is these institutions which will set the models that will be imitated by much of the world.

We are now entering a period of transition as significant as the transition from an agricultural to an industrial society. Whether it is labeled the "information society" or given any other name, it will require a new set of management priorities and practices. The relationship between the employee, the organization, and the manager will be remade. It will be a relationship built on trust and personal responsibility. It will require a new ethic and a new spirit. And in this new spirit we can all take pride, for it will represent the integration of the interests of the individual and those of the productive institution. The conditions that lead to personal fulfillment are becoming the same conditions that lead to corporate productivity. Personal responsibility, rewards for achievement, close relationships with respected peers, continual learning, and involvement in decision making will all be characteristics of the organization of the future.

Similarly, the age-old dichotomy between the material and the spiritual will give way to integration. The values of the organization and the collective spirit of its members will be directly related to its material attainment. In the age we are entering, the employee will dedicate his efforts and perform to his or her best ability when the values and behavior of the organization are worthy of that dedication.

An organization is much like a living organism. Its functions and structure are much like the body's. Its actions may be either intelligent or stupid. Its adherence to a consistent set of beliefs, a "good," higher in scope and priority than any short-term decision or action, which exerts overriding influence on all actions, is its soul. In our secular society we have segmented our lives into matters concerned with material pursuit and matters of the spirit. We have even looked upon the pursuit of material gain as inherently counter to the attainment of spiritual values. The poor and those who reject our wealth-producing institutions for ideological reasons are viewed as claimants to a more noble spirit. This is a false delusion. On the contrary, it is those who bear the burden of production, who are responsible for the creation of the wealth and permit the leisure and education our society allows, these are the ones who are making the noble contribution.

Management is rediscovering its soul. America's best corporations and best managers are debating the values upon which their corporate cultures are built. They are recognizing the link between values, behavior, and productivity. They are shaping their corporate cultures to elicit the best loyalties, creative energies, and business performance possible. We are all fortunate to be living in an age in which this transition to maturity is being attained. For within this integration rest our best hopes for a society that serves both our material and spiritual needs.

Notes

CHAPTER 1

1. The Business Week Team. *The Reindustrialization of America*. New York: McGraw-Hill Book Company, 1982, p. 11.
2. Ibid, p. 8.
3. Toynbee, Arnold. *A Study of History*. New York: Oxford University Press, 1962.
4. Muller, Herbert J. *The Uses of the Past*. New York: Oxford University Press, 1952, pp. 226–243.
5. Carcopino, Jerome. *Daily Life in Ancient Rome*. New Haven and London: Yale University Press, 1940, pp. 76–95.
6. Muller, p. 229.

CHAPTER 2

1. Drucker, Peter. *Management: Tasks, Practices, Responsibilities*. New York: Harper & Row, 1974, p. 74.
2. Pascale, Richard Tanner, and Anthony G. Athos. *The Art of Japanese Management*. New York: Simon & Schuster, 1981, pp. 177–188.
3. Ibid, p. 184.
4. Reich, Robert B. *The Next American Frontier*. New York: Times Books, 1983, pp. 140–141.
5. Ibid. p. 157.

6. Livesay, Harold C. *American Made: Men Who Shaped the American Economy.* Boston: Little, Brown & Company, 1979, p. 123.
7. Note: The term "The Metal Company" is used to protect the anonymity of the actual firm.
8. Novak, Michael. *The Spirit of Democratic Capitalism.* New York: Simon & Schuster, 1982, p. 31.
9. Drucker, pp. 9–10.

CHAPTER 3
1. Cox, Allan. *The Cox Report on the American Corporation.* New York: Delacorte Press, 1982, pp. 36–38.

CHAPTER 5
1. Drucker, Peter. *The Unseen Revolution: How Pension Fund Socialism Came to America.* New York: Harper & Row, 1976.

CHAPTER 7
1. *People and Productivity: A Challenge to Corporate America.* New York: New York Stock Exchange, Inc., 1982.
2. Christopher, Robert C. *The Japanese Mind: The Goliath Explained.* New York: Linden Press, Simon & Schuster, 1983, p. 79.
3. Deming, W. Edwards. *Quality, Productivity, and Competitive Position.* Cambridge: Massachusetts Institute of Technology Center for Advanced Engineering Study, 1982.
4. Ibid., p. 119.
5. Ibid., p. 158.
6. Peters, Thomas J., and Robert H. Waterman. *In Search of Excellence.* New York: Harper & Row, 1982.

CHAPTER 8
1. Mason Mills and the other names in this story are fictitious.
2. Bowles, Samuel, David M. Gordon, and Thomas E. Weisskopf. *Beyond the Waste Land.* New York: Anchor Press, Doubleday, 1983.

CHAPTER 9

1. MacGregor Burns, James. *Leadership*. New York: Harper & Row, 1978, p. 18.
2. Schmidt, Warren H., and Barry Z. Posner. *Managerial Values and Expectations*. New York: The American Management Associations, 1982.
3. Cox, Allan. *The Cox Report on the American Corporation*. New York: Delacorte Press, 1982, pp. 326–327.
4. Tannenbaum, Robert, and Warren H. Schmidt. "How to Choose a Leadership Pattern," in *Executive Success: Making It in Management*. New York: John Wiley & Sons, 1983.
5. Ohmann, O. A. "Skyhooks—With Special Implications for Monday Through Friday," in *Executive Success: Making It in Management*. New York: John Wiley & Sons, 1983.

CHAPTER 10

1. Tichy, Noel, Charles Fombrun, and Mary Ann Devanna. "Strategic Human Resource Management," a working paper, July, 1981. And Tichy, Noel. "Managing Change Strategically: The Technical, Political and Cultural Keys." *Organizational Dynamics*. Autumn, 1982. New York: American Management Associations, p. 59.
2. Devanna, Mary Ann. "Human Resource Management: A Strategic Perspective." *Organizational Dynamics*, Winter, 1981. New York: American Management Associations, p. 51.
3. Porter, Michael. *Competitive Strategy: Techniques for Analyzing Industries and Competitors*. New York: The Free Press, 1980.

CHAPTER 13

1. Miller, Lawrence M. *Behavior Management: The New Science of Managing People at Work*. New York: John Wiley & Sons, 1978.
2. Zemke, Ron, and Thomas Kramlinger. *Figuring Things Out: A Trainer's Guide to Needs and Task Analysis*. Reading, Mass.: Addison-Wesley Publishing Company, 1982.
3. Miller, p. 242.
4. Skinner, B. F. *Science and Human Behavior*. New York: The Free Press, 1953.

5. Frederiksen, Lee W. *Handbook of Organizational Behavior Management*. New York: John Wiley & Sons, 1982.
6. Deal, Terrence E., and Allan A. Kennedy. *Corporate Cultures: The Rites and Rituals of Corporate Life*. Reading, Mass.: Addison-Wesley Publishing Company, 1982.